PRAIRIE FLYERS OF CENTRAL ILLINOIS

A CENTURY OF AVIATION IN AMERICA'S HEARTLAND

EDITH BRADY-LUNNY, DENIS HAMBUCKEN
AND JOHN WARNER

Published by The History Press
An imprint of Arcadia Publishing
Charleston, SC
www.historypress.com

All images are from family and authors' collections, unless otherwise credited.

Cover: May 1928. Vernelle "Red" Irwin stands before his Curtiss JN-4 Jenny, flanked by parents Minnie and Wilbur; the photo records his first landing on the family farm in Hallsville, Illinois.

First published 2025

Manufactured in the United States

ISBN 9781467159296

Library of Congress Control Number: 2025934493

For John Warner, our dear friend and prairie flyer, who left us much too soon.

CONTENTS

ACKNOWLEDGEMENTS

The authors are grateful to all the aviators and aviation enthusiasts whose stories we were fortunate to share, first with visitors to our museum exhibit and later with readers. We are grateful to the C.H. Moore Homestead and DeWitt County Museum, and its director Joey Long, for giving us the opportunity to put together the "Prairie Flyers" exhibit in Clinton, Illinois. The experience introduced us to the remarkable people who played a role in aviation in America's heartland. We also thank Maureen and Jonah Kolb for their support and the families of our interview subjects who shared their stories, artifacts and photos to help us better tell the stories.

We acknowledge the thoughtful editing and guidance we have received from The History Press that has brought the *Prairie Flyers* story to an audience of aviation and history lovers.

Prologue

PLANES ON THE PLAINS

The desire to fly is an idea handed down to us by our ancestors who, in their grueling travels across trackless lands in prehistoric times, looked enviously on the birds soaring freely through space, at full speed, above all obstacles, on the infinite highway of the air.

It's no coincidence that Wilbur and Orville Wright, two brothers who grew up in Ohio, heard and answered the timeless call from the heavens. It's not mere chance that so many of our aviation pioneers are kids from the heartland of our nation—country kids, farm kids, small-town kids—who grew up accustomed to and familiar with our vast expanses of earth and sky. They looked aloft and dreamed.

Walter Beech grew up in Tennessee. He first flew in 1905, at fourteen years old, in a glider he designed and built all by himself. During World War I, he was a pilot in the United States Army Air Service. In 1924, Beech, Clyde Cessna and Lloyd Stearman formed Travel Air Manufacturing Company, producing some of the finest American aircraft of the period. In 1932, with his wife, Olive, and one other partner, Walter Beech formed Beech Aircraft Company in Wichita, Kansas. The company grew into one of the "big three" (Beechcraft, Cessna and Piper) general aviation manufacturers of the twentieth century. Still based on the prairie outside Wichita, nowadays Beechcraft is a division of Textron Aviation.

Clyde Cessna was born in Iowa and came of age way out on the southwest plains of Kansas in the little farm town of Rago. An aerial exhibition in 1910 was all it took for Clyde; he was hooked on the idea of becoming a pilot. A farm kid, he had some mechanical ability, and building his own airplane was the only way he could afford to fly. Cessna worked for a while for the Queen Aeroplane Company in New York, staying just long enough to learn the basics of aircraft construction and save a few paychecks. Then he went back to the Midwest, this time Oklahoma, to design and build his first airplane in 1911.

Cessna taught himself to fly out there on the Kansas prairies, but he crashed and rebuilt his ship thirteen times before finally getting the job done; along the way, he learned nearly every aspect of aircraft design and engineering. When he mastered flight, Clyde Cessna entered the aviation history books as the first person to build and fly an airplane anywhere between the Mississippi and the Rocky Mountains. In 1925, Cessna joined Walter Beech and Lloyd Stearman in the formation of Travel Air Manufacturing Company. In 1927, he formed Cessna Aircraft Corporation. The company continues to this day as a leader in the production of general aviation aircraft.

Amelia Earhart was born and raised in Atchison, Kansas, and grew up in Des Moines, Iowa. She took her first flight at age twenty-three. "By the time I had got to two or three thousand feet off the ground, I knew I had to fly," she later recalled.

In 1928, Earhart became the first female passenger to cross the Atlantic by airplane. In 1932, she made a second trip, this time piloting a Lockheed Vega 5B—the first woman to make a nonstop flight across the Atlantic. "Aviation, this young modern giant, exemplifies the possible relationships of women with the creations of science," Earhart wrote.

Earhart's flying career brought her to Purdue University, where she joined the faculty as an advisor to aeronautical engineering students and a career counselor to the female students in the program. By the time she and navigator Fred Noonan disappeared over the Atlantic in their Lockheed Electra in 1937, Earhart was a member of the National Woman's Party and an early supporter of the Equal Rights Amendment.

Matthew Laird grew up in Chicago. After watching Walter Brooks pilot a Wright Flyer in Grant Park, Laird later recalled, "I was so thrilled with seeing him fly and maneuver around the land that I said right then and there that I wanted part of it and made up my mind I was going to have it. I didn't know how, but I would."

Laird built his first full-size aircraft at age fifteen: a bicycle with glider wings. Then he designed and built a monoplane in his mom's attic and flew it for the first time on September 15, 1913. He used the little ship to teach himself to fly.

In 1920, Laird established the E.M. Laird Aviation Company in Wichita, Kansas. Lloyd Stearman and Walter Beech were among the company's employees, and Clyde Cessna was among the first to buy his product.

The company gained a reputation for high-quality aircraft that were sleek, rugged and fast. Laird had the ability to generate more speed with less horsepower than other designers, primarily due to the quality of his company's workmanship, and his thinking set the pattern for an American way of designing aircraft that continues to this day.

Charles "Slim" Lindbergh grew up in the wide-open country of Minnesota. He started flying lessons in 1922 and soloed in 1923 in a surplus Curtiss JN-4 "Jenny" that he had purchased for $500. After barnstorming across the country for several months, he joined the U.S. Army Air Service in 1924. Only 18 of the 104 cadets completed the program when Lindbergh graduated first in the class in 1925.

After that, he took a flying job with Robertson Aircraft Corporation in St. Louis, where he laid out the nation's first airmail route between St. Louis and Chicago. Lindbergh hauled the mail from St. Louis to Chicago and back again, making night flights over the pastures and farms and timber claims of the Illinois prairie.

By the time he went after the Orteig Prize—a $25,000 prize offered by Raymond Orteig for the first successful nonstop flight between New York and Paris—in May 1927, Lindbergh had already logged hundreds of hours of flying alone over the vast, coal-black Illinois darkness, navigating by the stars. He took off from Roosevelt Field and, after thirty-three and a half hours aloft, touched down without incident at Le Bourget airfield in Paris. The prairies of the Midwest had prepared Lindbergh for his task.

Eddie Rickenbacker was born in Columbus, Ohio, in 1890. Like so many kids out on the prairie in those days, Rickenbacker worshipped at the altar of the God Motor. For him, the allure of the skies came in the form of a question: how to travel vast distances with ease. To Rickenbacker, the answer was speed, and he got into the air by way of automobile racing. When his dad died unexpectedly, Eddie dropped out of seventh grade and went to work. He picked up mechanical engineering through a correspondence course. After landing a job at Harvey Firestone's car company, Rickenbacker started racing cars. Just plainly good at speed, he quickly garnered a national reputation as a racing driver.

With the approach of World War I, Rickenbacker shared an idea with a *New York Times* reporter: "War would practically put a stop to racing, and we have a training that our country would need in the time of war. We are experts in judging speed and in motor knowledge."

The U.S. Army made Rickenbacker chief engineer for an American airbase in France. While supervising the construction of the U.S. Air

Service training field in Issoudin, Rickenbacker learned to fly. Aerobatics made him airsick, so every day he took himself aloft and flew every kind of aerobatic maneuver, over and over again, until he finally got over being ill.

Before World War I, there were all sorts of theories about what could be made of "combat airpower," if there even was such a thing, and when he became commander of the American 94th Aero Squadron in France, Eddie Rickenbacker pioneered American aerial warfare. He chose pilots for his squadron who were bright and alert—a cut above the rest—and formed a proud, elite group of flyers. As a commander, Rickenbacker was stern but fair, a leader who never asked anything of his flyers that he couldn't, or wouldn't, do himself. With twenty-six victories at war's end, Rickenbacker came home the top-ranked pilot in the American military, an American "ace of aces," a gifted, innovative aviator of superior ability—a quintessential American hero. He was admired and respected by aviators around the world and enjoyed international presence and popularity. Eddie Rickenbacker set a standard for American military combat aviators that continues today.

Rickenbacker wasn't finished with flying when he came home. In 1938, he acquired Eastern Airlines, a struggling, short-haul carrier, and transformed it into a major commercial airline with an international reputation of excellence. He collaborated with aircraft designers to produce larger, faster airliners like the Lockheed Constellation and the Douglas DC-4. The standards and ways of doing business at Eastern Airlines became guidelines for other airlines all over the globe.

Born of the Sun

All that space out there on our prairies—that's what does it. In the United States, there is more space with nothing in it than there is with anything in it. That's what makes America what it is. America's plains and prairies foster a sense of freedom, an urging of ingenuity and opportunity. Hope has always been among the promises of our open spaces, and people live there with a palpable sense that tomorrow can be better than today. Out there on our plains and prairies, there's a feeling that anything goes.

Out on our prairies, out on our Great Plains, American kids grow up with Mother Nature at arm's length. Kids on the prairies learn astronomy by stepping outside and studying the stars; the planets make a permanent map in their minds. Prairie kids are botanists and meteorologists at age ten, an expression of their intimate association with earth and sky. Only a mile from the house, the vastness of nature awaits. They are always in touch with Mother Nature's handiwork.

Out on our plains and prairies, an enormous sky garden offers inspiration on a daily basis. Towering, majestic cloud formations that conjure up fairy tale images, sunsets and sunrises in breathtaking pastels of azure and gold, galaxies of stars in the nighttime sky—kids on our plains live in common with magnificence. And all they need to do is look up. West of the Appalachian Mountains, government surveyors came first and measured and quantified the land along cardinal points. They laid out our plains in a square-mile checkerboard that stretches as far as the eye can see. After the surveyors left, the people came and filled up the country.

In a wide-open country, it's helpful to have a reliable reference to the cardinal points of North, South, East and West. For children of the prairie, the surveyors' grid work forms a map in their minds, and they grow up with an innate, unerring sense of direction. Midwesterners and westerners think in terms of cardinal points and give directions like they are looking at a compass: "Follow this road north for three miles. Your destination will be on the east side of the road."

In open country, there's a landing field just about everywhere—no trees to avoid and no obstacles to clear—and a person can imagine coming and going with no difficulty. The ability to travel vast distances with ease comes frequently to mind, alluring, inviting and intriguing in its appeal. Navigating across uninhabited spaces is second nature to people out on the plains; flying across the country in an airplane doesn't feel like too much of a stretch. Out on the plains, for those who hear her call in the winds, for those who read her message in the skies, for those who dream, Mother Nature's invitation is constant and insistent.

Out there on the prairies, the sky, a field, a plane—it all seems so possible.

They Traveled a Short While Toward the Sun

In 2022, we were fortunate to work with the C.H. Moore Homestead and DeWitt County Museum in Clinton, Illinois, to create "Prairie Flyers: A Century of Aviation in DeWitt County." Our premise was simple: If you aren't into airplanes, you haven't heard the remarkable aviation stories that come from right here in your very own backyard.

We set out to tell people in the county about their very own friends and neighbors. We conducted local interviews and gathered artifacts and souvenirs. We visited with men and women of all ages and backgrounds, all of whom had been drawn to aviation in some way and had stories to tell. Our stories started with the county's aviation pioneers and progressed to today's flyers. There were pilots and copilots, ground personnel, engineers and astronomers, mechanics, civilian flyers, meteorologists, commercial pilots and military aviators. One interview led to another; the more we looked, the more we found.

Yet when the exhibit ended, when everyone had the chance to consider and reflect, several matters became very clear. First, although our exhibit focused on flying in central Illinois, the plains and prairies of our nation contribute very powerfully to the larger story of aviation. Our prairies and plains were the first region to be settled after the American Revolution. There's a hands-on, "can do" spirit to the region that survives to this day. When Mother Nature made our prairies, she created one vast airfield. America's heartland has always called people to the sky and always will.

Second, the "Prairie Flyers" temporary exhibit and catalogue barely scratched the surface. All of the states in our nation's midsection are just naturally conducive to flying; instances of aviation history can be found just about everywhere. We followed many leads and uncovered so many additional stories. The only way to do them all justice was to broaden our scope and begin again. This book is the result of our efforts.

Finally, America's love affair with aviation is ardent and strong, very much alive, and American aviation is a work in progress. It's an unfinished story. Every day, somehow, somewhere, another page is being written. Even our expanded collection of stories is just today's montage, like the daily footage of an epic movie (complete with heroes and heroines, knights in shining armor and fire-breathing dragons) that is still being filmed. We offer a freeze frame, a snapshot, a moment in time.

We pay homage to all American flyers, living or dead, who heard and answered the call from the skies.

Near the snow, near the sun, in the highest fields,
See how their names are feted by the waving grass
And by the streamers of white cloud
And whispers of wind in the listening sky.
The names of those who in their lives fought for life, who wore at their hearts the fire's center.
Born of the sun they travelled a short while towards the sun, and left the vivid air signed with their honor.

—*Stephen Spender*

SHIRLEY BUSH

ARMY AIR SERVICE

Shirley Bush was looking for an alternative to high school when he left Clinton with a group of buddies for Peoria to join the Army Air Service. Everyone was accepted except the sixteen-year-old Bush, who was sent home to gain at least ten pounds.

In his written account of his boyhood years growing up in a family of thirteen children, Bush recalled his disappointment and how he overcame the rejection. "The next month, I worked and ate anything I could get a hold of. When the month was up, I went by the grocery store and got a big sack of bananas and got on the interurban and ate all of them before I went to Peoria. I passed that time with 10 pounds to spare."

Assigned in 1924 to Selfridge Field in Mount Clemens, Michigan, Bush joined the squadron members, who were learning to make parachute jumps. In two weeks, he could fold his chute and summoned the nerve to make the jump. "I did not sleep well that night. I was about to back out. But the guys kept teasing me and I did want to be one of the bunch. So that afternoon, when I finished my duty for the day, I went out to the hangar and there was a trainer plane about ready to take off. Just a two-seater. I got in the backseat, and we went up to 3500 feet," Bush wrote in his journal.

There was no turning back. "The pilot slowed the engine as much as he could for me to get out. Boy was I weak. I don't know how I pushed myself over the side, but I did. That ground looked so far away. I don't think I ever counted to five so fast and pulled the ripcord. After that I began to breathe again."

Relief swept over Bush once he was safely inside the parachute pick-up vehicle. "I was sure glad that was over, and I said to myself, 'never again.'" The chance to ride in a biplane came after Bush agreed to keep the two-seater aircraft clean for a second lieutenant. "One day he asked if I wanted to learn how to operate a plane. We sat in the hangar, and I learned what made the plane fly up and down and bank to the right and left and read the instrument panels. After a few days of that, he started showing me in the air. It took several trips before I could fly it to suit him."

Army rules barred Bush from taking off or landing the plane, but his instructor gave him passing grades for operating in the air.

A notice on the bulletin board offering transfers to the lighter-than-air station at Scott Field in Belleville, Illinois, piqued Bush's interest. One month later, he was pushing a broom in an airship hangar large enough to hold 100,000 men—nearly the size of the U.S. Army in 1923. The task of sweeping the hangar took twenty men half a day.

The Army Balloon and Airship School was transferred in 1921 from Brooks Fields, Texas, to the airfield in southern Illinois. Aerial photography and meteorology research and altitude experiments were conducted on the base. The army used TAs (Training, Type A), non-rigid airships, for pilot training. The training models were the first army airships designed for helium inflation.

The TA-1 and TA-2 were 162 feet long, 39.3 feet in diameter, 53.5 feet high and 49 feet wide. The 130,600 cubic feet of helium provided an endurance of 8.7 hours and a range of 390 miles. During his time at the lighter-than-air station, Bush took three dirigible rides. "It was sure different than an airplane. Just like flowing through the air and very quiet, too."

With a top speed of about fifty miles per hour, the rides lasted three to four hours over St. Louis and southern portions of Illinois and Missouri. "It was a wonderful view," Bush recalled.

Several records were set during the lighter-than-air era spanning sixteen years at Scott Field. A seventy-four-mile-per-hour speed record for dirigibles was set in 1923 by the TC-1, and the American free balloon altitude of 28,510 feet was set in 1927.

Opposite: Shirley Bush.

Above: Bush took three flights on the TA-1 Training Airship at Scott Field in southern Illinois.

The use of airships diminished in the late 1920s as the military shifted to balloons. The 1st Balloon Company replaced the 12th Airship Company in 1929. Airplanes took over activities at Scott Field by the mid-1930s. A series of fatal airship accidents, including the 1925 crash of the navy's USS *Shenandoah* that killed fourteen crew members, put an end to the lighter-than-air program in May 1937.

Bush returned to his family in Clinton after he left the service. He became a house painter, and he and his wife, Elsie, operated two grocery stores. In 1943, Bush received a draft notice and joined the U.S. Navy Seebees. His travels took him to Japan, where he saw the aftermath of two nuclear bombs dropped by the United States. "Words just cannot picture how the area looked. Everything was leveled," Bush wrote.

After his death in 1992, Bush was remembered as a grandfather with a quick smile and a ready supply of candy and soda pop. The stories of his military service and the hardships that were all part of his determination to make a living were revealed in his writing. "Grandpa led a very interesting life. I learned more about him after his death and in his own writings. But to me, he was my fun, loving, quiet and slightly mischievous Grandpa. And he was one of us," wrote Cindy Rockhold, Bush's granddaughter.

LEE GEHLBACH

TEST PILOT

Skilled and fearless, Lee Gehlbach pushed the bounds of aviation as a test pilot with a penchant for adventure.

Born in 1902 on a farm between Beason and Waynesville, Gehlbach enlisted in the U.S. Army Air Service after graduation from the University of Illinois with an aeronautical degree. He spent three years with the 1st Pursuit Group at Selfridge Field in Michigan. Training as a military test pilot taught Gehlbach how to fly planes in ways most people could not imagine. Not only did he perform the death-defying moves, he also lived to talk about it.

"I'll fly anything, anytime, anywhere, for money, marbles or chalk," the DeWitt County native once said of his career as a legendary test pilot. Starting in 1929, Gehlbach went to work as an engineer and test pilot for several aircraft companies. He was chief test pilot for the Great Lakes Aircraft Corporation.

Gehlbach began collecting top honors as a racing pilot in 1930 with his first-place trophy in the All-American Air Derby, flying a monoplane nicknamed the "Little Rocket." Gehlbach flew 5,541 miles and took first place with 43 hours, 35 minutes and 40 seconds of flying time. His average speed was 127.1 miles per hour.

The former army pilot collected the $15,000 derby purse in Detroit after finishing ahead of eighteen other flyers. The seven-thousand-mile race around the United States and into Mexico put Gehlbach on the pages of newspapers from coast to coast.

Gehlbach was dubbed "America's No. 1 Test Pilot" in a 1936 magazine advertisement for Camel cigarettes.

At thirty-two, Gehlbach's "minor injuries to the head" were reported in the *New York Times* after he parachuted from eight thousand feet when his plane started to break up during a test run. He walked away from the crumpled aircraft.

Gehlbach solidified his reputation as a crack test pilot when he managed to survive a test flight of a beefed-up version of the Grumman bomber that killed renowned pilot Jimmy Collins. Gehlbach and Collins were part of an elite group of pilots known as the "Suicide Club," a reference to their willingness to test navy dive bombers. The power dives from twenty thousand feet with the motor at full throttle amazed even the most experienced pilots watching from the ground.

In 1935, a navy observer described Gehlbach's effort to pull a single-seater experimental aircraft out of a tailspin. "Using an old pilot's trick, he even stood upright in the cockpit, hoping the wind pressure on his body would right the plane. Finally at 2,000 feet, with the earth rushing at him at 200 feet a second, he bailed out and descended easily while the plane hurtled into a nearby pine tree."

The dashing and daring pilot attracted the attention of the makers of Camel cigarettes, who dubbed him "America's No. 1 Test Pilot" in a 1936 advertisement for the tobacco brand. "You know, chance is only ten percent of my business. Keeping alert and in fine condition is the other ninety percent."

Gehlbach's friends and neighbors in central Illinois were among the first to witness his exploits in aerobatics. According to one story, Gehlback and fellow pilot Red Irwin tied the wings of two biplanes together for a

Gehlbach was known for flying the notoriously dangerous Granville Gee Bee R6.

stunt session at Hooterville Airport, Irwin's airport near Hallsville. When asked why he took up aeronautical engineering, Gehlbach told a reporter that he was "a farmer's son who couldn't get used to getting up at 4 in the morning."

Gehlbach was a familiar face around Lincoln, where he flew in for visits and landed in an open field outside of town. He was generous with offers of rides to friends and visitors to the Logan County Fair.

Gehlbach died in 1975 in Lincoln, where he lived after his retirement.

VERNELLE "RED" IRWIN

STUNT PILOT, OIL COMPANY EXECUTIVE

For many flyers the aviation bug bites early, and it bites hard. Vernelle "Red" Irwin of Hallsville, Illinois, caught the infection when he was just a kid, ten or twelve years old, after taking his first plane ride in August 1920, at the local county fair. "I never got it out of my system," he said many years later in conversations with John Warner, who later purchased Irwin's airport. "From that day on I always wanted to fly."

Red took a ride with a barnstormer—the most sensational entertainment to be found in the early days of aviation. Barnstormers were just pilots trying to make a living with an airplane, flying around the country selling rides and doing stunts. At first, barnstorming pilots worked alone, but gradually they became professional entertainers who worked together in troupes that they called "flying circuses." As a routine that impressed people with a pilot's skill and the sturdiness of the airplane, barnstorming was extremely popular all across the country in the 1920s. It was the first expression of civilian aviation in the history of flight. Barnstorming pilots became celebrities, the rock stars of their day, with fans who followed their every move. Even Charles Lindbergh began his flying career as a barnstormer.

The pilot took young Red up and wrung him out. In loops, spins and rolls, he threw his airplane all over the sky. Other passengers might have gotten sick or frightened, but not Red Irwin. He was mesmerized, loved it, couldn't wait for more! In that simple ride at a summer fair, the young man found his calling.

Red Irwin.

When people get infected by the aviation bug, the symptoms are easy to spot. They swing in a backyard swing and daydream about flying. They build model airplanes. They lie on their backs in the yard and study the clouds. At the slightest sound from aloft, they scan the sky like they're looking for a lost dog. They follow every airplane news story, devour every book and magazine about flying, loaf around at airports and talk about airplanes to anyone who will listen.

"I was in the spring of my first year in college," recalled Red, "when Lindbergh hopped across the ocean. My college advisor told me that I was crazy—that aviation would never amount to anything."

So, after studying engineering at the University of Illinois, where courses on aviation were conspicuously absent, Red withdrew from the college. Instead, on February 24, 1928, he invested $35.00 to join the Bloomington Flying Club. Flying lessons were furnished to members at $2.50 an hour, and on February 25, 1928, Red took his first hour of instruction. Red's dad, Wilbur Irwin, furnished the $37.50 for his son's membership and first hour of schooling. Said Red, "It was so cold that day my face got frost-bitten."

"I flew for a couple of years before there were any regulations—didn't even have to keep track of my flight time," Red remarked. In 1928, there were no aviation rules or regulations of any sort. There were no physical standards or qualifications for flyers to meet. There were no regulations mandating flight instruction, and there was no such thing as a pilot's license. There were no maintenance requirements for the aircraft either. "A lot of people just flew. They didn't take lessons. They just got their hands on an airplane and taught themselves to fly it. There's an old superstition that it's bad luck to have your picture taken in front of your airplane on your very first flight. That's because for many flyers in those days their first flight was also their last flight."

"Many men joined the air service to learn to fly," Red explained. "Or they started flying and then joined the service in order to become better pilots. I didn't want to be a service pilot like Lee Gehlbach. I just wanted to fly. An old army pilot was my flight instructor. He let me fly solo after three hours in the air. When I had ten hours of flight time, my instructor quit. I was the high-time pilot on the field and became flight instructor."

May 1928 brought the first aircraft landings at Hallsville. Red piloted a Curtiss JN-4D "Jenny" that belonged to the Bloomington Flying Club. The Jenny was the primary aircraft used by the United States to train pilots in World War I. It was constructed from wood and covered with linen fabric. Metal was used only for wing tips, wing trailing edges, engines and engine mounts, landing gear components and miscellaneous hardware. The plane had exposed struts and interlacing brace wires, and flyers nicknamed it the "flying birdcage."

"I've always thought of that old Jenny as the aeronautical equivalent of a Model T Ford," Red remarked years later. "In the early twenties the government auctioned off a large number of Jennies. This was when the training fields were closing. The aircraft changed hands for whatever they would bring. I always heard that those Jennies went at auction for as little as $50.00 apiece. The Flying Club owned a surplus Jenny. On the civilian market you could buy a Jenny, fully equipped and with a brand-new OX-5 engine, for about $500.00. Pretty cheap for an airplane!" The Jenny was designed by Glenn Curtiss and powered by an OX-5 engine.

"At idle on the ground, you could see the propeller ticking over. Straight and level it would cruise at seventy to seventy-five miles per hour. You could slow fly it at about 45 mph. It would climb at about 200 feet per minute. I mostly flew about 700 feet above the ground. It took too much time and gasoline to climb any higher."

The OX-5 was a V-8, water-cooled, four-stroke engine that developed ninety horsepower at 1400rpm. It burned nine gallons of gasoline per hour. The crankcase held four gallons of oil. The rocker arms were exposed, clattering loudly and spewing oil whenever the engine ran.

"The old timers used to say that if it wasn't blowing oil, the OX-5 wasn't running right. We wore silk scarves to wipe the oil from our goggles. We wore flight suits to stay clean. You could always tell a high-time pilot by the oil splattered all over his coveralls. The engine was lubricated with castor oil and after a few days flying behind it, a pilot inhaled so much oil and absorbed so much oil through his skin that he got diarrhea and had to stop flying until he tightened up."

The Jenny handled sluggishly and required the pilot's constant attention to the controls. It flew through the air like a log wagon and persistently sought to veer left. With two passengers, it became so tail heavy that the nose never ceased to try to point straight up. A few minutes at the controls left the pilot's right hand and arm aching and his right leg tense from correcting the aircraft's tendency to turn left. "A few hours flying a Jenny would qualify any pilot to fly an amphibian, a tri-motor or a seaplane," Red said later.

After he soloed in Bloomington, Red made his flying visit to Hallsville, heading directly south to Clinton and then turning west toward home. When he landed in his family's clover field at Hallsville, Red caused a riot—almost the entire village came running.

Wilbur Irwin was at home at the time, out in the backyard, hoeing potatoes in his garden. He heard the airplane when it flew over. He even watched for a few minutes as it banked and soared.

"Don't you want to see the aeroplane?" yelled a neighbor hurrying past.

"Nope," replied the gardener.

"Why not? Your boy's a'flyin' it!" Wilbur guessed he would look after all!

Everyone, the entire village, gathered around to look. Red stood with his folks in front of the Jenny, and a neighbor snapped a picture.

Airplanes must always take off and land into the wind. In the early days, airports were large circular fields so that flyers could take off and land into whatever direction the wind was strongest. Chicago's O'Hare Airport began life as a circular cinder landing field adjacent to a large apple orchard and was known as "Orchard Field." O'Hare Airport's three letter identifier, ORD, traces the field's history back to those early days.

When Red began flying to and from Hallsville, he took off and landed in every direction. It all depended on the direction of the wind. He took off and landed from every available location too. Sometimes he flew from

Red Irwin stands with family members around his Travel Air Model 4000. Parents Minnie and Wilbur are alongside; fiancée Ruth Sutter stands behind him on a tire.

his family's farm. Sometimes he flew from his uncle's farm across the road. Sometimes he flew from the north side of the village and sometimes from the south side. It all depended on the condition of the fields.

In the early 1930s, Red bought a Travel Air Model 4000, a two-place open-cockpit biplane powered by a three-hundred-horsepower Wright engine. Travel Air was a premier aircraft company, and its Model 4000 ranked among the finest aircraft in the world. It was much too valuable to sit outside in the elements.

A shed at his grandparents' house became Red's first airplane hangar.

STUNTING BY ACCIDENT

Red's initiation into the world of stunt flying came by accident. "I was flying over Kenney, hauling passengers, when I made too tight a turn and went into a tailspin. By instinct I got out of it. I didn't know what I had done—that it was a tailspin—until I was on the ground and a World War I veteran came over and told me it was the prettiest tailspin he'd ever seen. I got sick to my stomach."

"The old Jenny had very few instruments," Red began another story. "A tachometer, an altimeter, an oil pressure gauge and a magnetic compass were all I had. Attitude indicators and turn coordinators hadn't even been invented back in those days, so a pilot had to look outside and level the wings against the horizon."

"Whenever I was in a steady climb," Red continued, "I saw that my tachometer indicated 1000 RPMs. One day I tried my luck at climbing through an overcast layer. I set the nose in a climb and entered the cloud deck. By keeping the tachometer at 1000 RPMs, I knew I was climbing. After a few seconds of no visibility, I popped out in the sunshine, above the clouds."

"When a plane is in a spin it always goes straight down," Red explained. "So, when I wanted to come back down through the clouds, I just kicked the plane into a spin. Down I went, and when the Jenny busted out of the bottom of the clouds, I just kicked it out of the spin and resumed straight and level flight."

"One day two boys from Hallsville saw me come down out of the clouds that way," Red continued the story, "and they asked for a ride. Both guys climbed into the front seat and up we went. After we had flown around up there for a while, I kicked the ship into a spin and we started down. When we broke out, I neutralized the stick and pushed opposite rudder. That's the way you get out of a spin. But nothing happened. We kept spinning, going straight down. I tried to recover again and nothing happened. The ground was rushing up to meet us."

"I don't know what made me think of this," Red spoke thoughtfully, "but I gave the ship full power and absolutely stomped on the right rudder. And with that, we came out of the spin."

"And you know…," Red said quietly, "the ground was Right There!" The weight of two passengers up front had put the little ship dangerously out of balance. The three were lucky to be alive. "After we landed, the boys wanted me to do it again. I was so scared, I got out and threw up. And I never tried that trick again."

Red was destined to be sick many more times. His stunting would no longer be an accident. He had to teach himself most of the stunts by the trial-and-error method. "In those days you weren't schooled in stunting. You had to go aloft and figure out all the maneuvers for yourself. To sum it up, really, I was lucky. More luck than brains. I did tricks I would never do today. Tricks that scared me."

People in DeWitt County grew accustomed to seeing Red Irwin flying above a freight train with his landing gear wheels resting on the roof of a boxcar. He liked to circle the clock tower on the courthouse in the center of Clinton's square. He flew down Clinton's streets so close to the ground that cars pulled over to get out of his way.

In Business

"Stunt flying was a way to make a living back in the '30s. You'd make $100.00 a show for five minutes work."

In the middle of the Depression, Red heard about a Ford Tri-motor airplane that was for sale for $1,200. The Ford Tri-motor was among America's earliest airliners. It had three engines—one on the nose and one on each wing. It had corrugated metal skin like a machine shed and carried twelve passengers.

"Once I bought the Tri-motor, I had to teach myself how to fly a multi-engine airplane. During takeoff, the two outboard engines had to be perfectly synchronized or the airplane would slew in one direction or the other, to the left or the right, depending upon which engine was running faster. In aerodynamics this condition is known as asymmetrical thrust." "I started my takeoff roll with only the center engine," Red explained. "Once the airplane was rolling straight, I applied power to the two outboard engines. That way I kept the engines properly balanced. It worked every time."

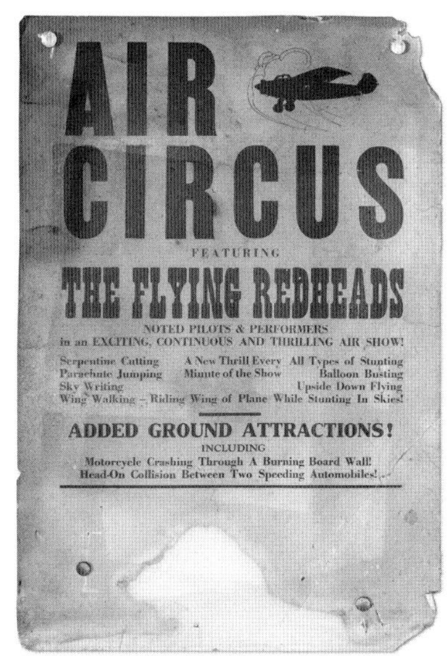

Irwin was one of the "Flying Redheads," a team of stunt flyers performing at airshows throughout the Midwest.

After Red flew the Tri-motor home to Hallsville, he realized that it was much too big to fit into his hangar. So Red taxied the big three-engine airplane into Hallsville and parked it next to his parents' house.

"The Tri-motor put me in business," Red recalled. "I had an advance man who would visit a town and obtain permission from a nearby farmer to land in his field. Then the advance man would put up hand bills advertising airplane rides for the next weekend. When the weekend came, we landed in the farmer's field and sold tickets for $2.50. People didn't have a lot of extra money in those days but they could always come up with the cash for an airplane ride."

"We would fill the plane and I would take off, circle town once so everyone could see their houses, and then I'd land," Red explained. "We averaged a new load of passengers every seven minutes. At the end, we paid the farmer and his family by giving them a free ride. It was common to clear $1,500 over a weekend. And during the depression that was a lot of money."

Old Pilots and Bold Pilots

There are two types of pilots—bold pilots and old pilots—but there are no old, bold pilots. "I decided I wanted to be an old pilot," Red remarked, "and in 1936 I became a pilot for Eastern Air Lines."

Eastern Air Lines was a major American airline from 1925 to 1991. The company came into prominence in about 1930 and for many years was headed by the World War I flying ace Eddie Rickenbacker. It had a near monopoly in air travel between New York and Florida from the 1930s until the 1950s and dominated the market for decades afterward. "I flew the Chicago to Newark route," Red recalled. "In those days the public was still anxious about air travel. If it was rainy or cloudy, people would cancel their reservations. Many times, I flew from Chicago to Newark with an empty airplane. Mr. Rickenbacker insisted that we fly the routes no matter what, to demonstrate the safety of aviation and the reliability of his airline company."

Eddie Rickenbacker was tough. When he was a young pilot in training, aerobatics made him seriously airsick. To get over his airsickness, he took himself aloft every day for two weeks and flew aerobatics—loops, spins, rolls and so forth. Rickenbacker threw up all over himself several times, but he kept at it until the airsickness subsided and the maneuvers no longer made him vomit.

The life of a professional pilot takes a toll on homes and marriages. During his years with Eastern Airlines, Red's marriage to his wife, Lillian, dissolved. In 1936, Red Irwin and Ruth Elton Sutter of Heyworth, Illinois, were married. In 1940, Red went to work for Mene Grande Oil Company, a division of Gulf Oil Company that operated in Venezuela.

"When I interviewed with Gulf in Venezuela," Red remembered, "two other job candidates and I were loaded on board a company airplane and flown around over the jungle. Every now and again, the company representative would point to a grass strip lying way down below. Some were small; some were on the edge of cliffs; some were bounded by trees. I told the company man that I could land on any of the fields that he'd shown to us. By the time we got back to the main airport, the other two pilots had withdrawn their applications."

"In South America, we were much more war conscious than people in the States seemed to be," Red recalled of the days leading up to the outbreak of World War II. "People in the States seemed too busy to notice. They just couldn't seem to see the forest for the trees. Down in South America we could back away and look at everything and get a better perspective." "I worked in Venezuela with a chip on my shoulder, hoping I'd get fired so that I could come back to the States and get into the Ferrying Command." But oil was critical to the American war effort. Red was informed that he was frozen to his South American pilot job for the duration.

"It wasn't easy to see out the war in a country where Americans are hated, but I did it," Red observed. "In my years in Venezuela I think I made about four friends I could really trust and depend upon."

Third Try

The stresses of South America took their toll on the Irwins. Red and his second wife, Ruth, quietly divorced, and she came back to the States alone. A relationship developed between Red and Charline McKinney, an Illinois girl he had known for years. They were married in Texas in 1947 and returned to Venezuela and Gulf Oil. This time around, the magic worked. Red and Charline were together until the end of their days.

Running an Airline

Major corporations all over the world have their own airlines. They own fleets of aircraft: passenger planes for traveling executives and employees, cargo planes for the transport of heavy equipment and so forth. They employ pilots and copilots, maintenance crews, ground handling crews, office staffs and even flight attendants. Corporate flight departments maintain flight schedules all over the globe, and employees of the company book their flights on their company's airline.

By war's end and well into the 1950s, Red Irwin managed the entire South American division of the Gulf Oil Company airline. He flew the first over-water route between Miami, Florida, and Caracas, Venezuela. "One night my wife and I were just sitting down to dinner when the manager of the Caracas airport called," Red recounted many years later. "'You'd better come down to the airport,' he told me. 'Two of your pilots have just landed a Gulf aircraft with the gear up.'"

"I went down to the airport and there on its belly on the runway was a shiny DC-3 in Gulf markings. The propellers were wrapped around the engine cowlings. Both pilots were just standing there with sheepish looks on their faces. I fired them both on the spot."

"Gulf aircraft were equipped with state-of-the-art autopilots," Red continued. "In the accident investigation we learned that the pilot and copilot didn't get along with each other. They had the airplane flying on its autopilot and they got into such an argument that they were rolling around on the floor in a fist fight. When they reached Caracas, the airplane didn't know any better and it just went ahead and landed itself on the autopilot. Of course, nobody in the cockpit was paying attention and nobody lowered the landing gear."

In 1958, Red was promoted to director of corporate aircraft for the entire Gulf Oil Company. The Irwins moved from Caracas, Venezuela, to Pittsburgh, Pennsylvania. From the Gulf Hangar at Allegheny County Airport in West Mifflin, Pennsylvania, Red Irwin went to work. Patterning himself after his old airline boss Eddie Rickenbacker, Red Irwin was hard and tough. He "talked the talk and walked the walk," developing one of the finest corporate flight operations in America. Yet at every opportunity he and his wife, Charline, came back to Hallsville and the family farm.

Petticoat Junction and *Green Acres* were popular television situation comedies that ran from 1963 through 1971. The stories were set in the fictional farm village of Hooterville, near the small farm town of Pixley. "Whenever

Charline and I came home on vacation," Red explained, "the staff at Gulf teased us about our trips to Hooterville. We played right along with their jokes. Everyone at Gulf was accustomed to seeing me in a business suit so my wife Charline had people in stitches when she told them that their boss wore bib overalls at home. And I told everyone that we lived at Hooterville Airport. About that time, we turned the old clover field into a sod runway, and I registered it with the FAA as 'Hooterville Airport.' It's been on all the aeronautical charts that way ever since." The Lockheed JetStar is a business jet produced from the early 1960s to the 1970s and was the first dedicated business jet to enter service. With a seating capacity of ten plus two crew, for many years the JetStar ranked among the largest business jets. It's distinguishable from other jets by its four engines mounted on the fuselage.

"Gulf Oil Company bought JetStars for their business flights," Red related. "A Lockheed test pilot was my instructor. When he learned that I used to barnstorm when I was younger, he really put me through my paces. We flew on four engines, then three engines, then two engines and finally, on just one engine. The JetStar is aerobatic, too. It will do loops and barrel rolls and snap rolls. I touched the wheels down once at Hooterville—a low pass—shattered windows in Hallsville."

A few years before Red's retirement, Gulf Oil Company arranged for the restoration of a classic Stearman open-cockpit biplane, to be flown by its barnstorming chief pilot and employed to advertise Gulf aviation products at airshows all over the country.

"A glossy custom Stearman streaked in, slick from cowled engine and wheel pants back to faired rudder and headrest," wrote Gordon Baxter for *Flying* magazine, describing the sensational 1972 Stearman fly-in in Galesburg, Illinois.

"Out of its cockpit there arose a most unlikely figure, like Faust coming up from Hell. First a great, red nose framed in white whiskers, and then the bulk of a magnificent paunch heaved upward. All of this balanced on the cockpit rim to unsheathe a pink, bald pate, and then it dropped to earth with surprising agility, like some giant Santa Claus, and was swept away by a throng of admirers."

Baxter continued, "'For God's sake, what was that?' I asked the little Italian chef with the Kaiser mustache who got out of the front hole. 'That's Red Irwin. He flies for Gulf Oil.' 'Flies what for Gulf Oil?' 'All of it. He's their chief corporate pilot and you are standing beside a mighty pricey Stearman. Look inside but be careful.' There, packed like jewels in black leather, was a full IFR panel. Instruments from crotch to chin, two of everything. When

Stearman 811 Golf calls Chicago Center and squawks ident, wouldn't you love to be there?"

Red's custom Stearman was black with gold wings and tail feathers and a gold stripe down the fuselage. The wing struts were chrome. The ship was powered by a 450-horsepower Pratt & Whitney radial engine that burned thirty gallons of 100-octane gasoline per hour. It cruised around 120 miles per hour. The airplane had an inverted oil and fuel system so Red could fly upside down for as long as he wanted. It had a smoke system, too, so Red could sky-write. The Stearman was a direct descendant of the old Travel Air biplanes and looked a lot like Red's Model 4000 from the early days. Red flew it like the old Travel Air too. When he retired, he based 811 Golf at Hooterville Airport and went back to his old tricks.

One quiet Sunday morning in the summer, Bob and Pat Leggett were driving home from Lincoln on State Route 10. Red was aloft in his Stearman and recognized their car. He swooped down behind them and touched the main wheels on the highway. Then he lifted off and touched the main wheels on the roof of the Leggetts' sedan. Then he flew ahead and touched the main wheels on the highway in front of them.

"If I'd had a gun, I could have shot him," Pat laughed.

Over at the field at Thorp Seed Company, Carl Thorp based a Beechcraft Bonanza. The Bonanza is a high-performance airplane with retractable landing gear and room for four. One summer day, Carl and Red flew it to a Flying Farmer's event in Iowa. They landed on a well-tended farm strip and spent the day.

"I flew over," Carl recalled, "and Red flew us back. By the time we were ready to leave, the day was hot and humid. There were two big oak trees down at the departure end of the runway and as we took off, it was obvious that we weren't going to clear the trees. I had no more than turned to Red and said 'We aren't going to clear the trees' when, within a wing's length of the ground, he rolled the plane 90 degrees and flew in between them."

Red Irwin's career in aviation took him from open-cockpit biplanes and clover fields to four-engine jets and International air travel. Yet after almost fifty years of flying everything, from Jennies to Jets, Irwin's first love—the open-cockpit biplane—remained his strongest.

"Any man that can make a living doing what he likes is lucky, and I'm that," Red always said of his life in the air.

WILLIAM SHIRLEY KARR

AERIAL PHOTOGRAPHER

From positions high above enemy lines and sensitive military installations, aerial photographers create maps and intelligence information that keep troops safe and informed during times of peace and conflict. In the summer of 1930, William Shirley Karr enlisted in the Army Air Corps, where he joined the ranks of pilots and aerial photographers. After initial training at Chanute Field in Rantoul, Karr was assigned to the 4th Photographic Section at Maxwell Field, Alabama.

The trip from the rural community of Wapella, Illinois, to Alabama was the longest trip the young, farm-raised recruit had ever made. The twenty-two-year-old requested a reassignment to the 12th Photographic Section at France Field in the Panama Canal Zone. The protection of the canal zone that linked the two oceans was the mission of troops assigned to the area. Air Corps photographers were part of observation squadrons that recorded topography, buildings, maps and terrain features useful in planning military maneuvers. Obvious defects in military efforts to conceal troop movements or equipment could also be detected in the aerial views. The camera lens also opened an opportunity for Karr to record historic visits to the region by celebrated aviators Charles Lindbergh and the final coast-to-coast voyage of the USS *Constitution*.

Karr's love of aerial photography did not end with his military service in 1934. The Abrams Aerial Survey Corporation in Lansing, Michigan, hired Karr as a photo-mapping technician. In 1940, he was named director and general manager of a second company known as Abrams Instrument Corporation. Karr would stay with Abrams until his retirement.

William Shirley Karr.

Karr's wide experience with various types of cameras, film processing and photogrammetry made him an asset for the Michigan firm. Partnering with Karr was Talbert Abrams, the company's founder, who became known as the "father of aerial photography." Abrams, a marine pilot in World War I, held a pilot's license signed by Orville Wright. He bought a surplus Curtiss JN-4 after the war and briefly worked as an airmail pilot. As a barnstormer, Abrams used his aerial photographs to attract paying passengers.

Abrams and Karr shared passions for flying and aerial photography. Both made a career of finding ways to expand the use of photogrammetry, the science of creating reliable measurements for surveying and mapmaking, commonly from aerial photography.

The Abrams Aircraft Corporation began work in 1937 to develop an aircraft that would improve things dramatically for aerial photographers forced to deal with oil leaks that affected the camera lens and unstable platforms ill-suited for their work.

The P-1 Explorer featured a clear nose of Plexiglas to give pilots an unobstructed view. A low-wing aluminum monoplane, the Explorer was constructed with a central pod for the pilot and camera gear. Delays in the redesign of the P-1 Explorer made it obsolete after World War II. The aircraft was later donated to the U.S. National Air and Space Museum. Karr's skills proved invaluable on a project that produced the Abrams Stereo Magnifier for the U.S. Army. The foldable map reading instrument provided a two-eye view of overlapping photos, giving interpreters better information for planning bombing missions and other operations. Karr, Abrams and Milford Moore are named on the December 30, 1942 patent application for the magnifier.

Abrams built other instruments to assist the military. In 1945, the Torpedo Camera Assessor was used on U.S. Navy TMB torpedo bombers. The device was designed to judge the results of torpedo attacks by providing photographs snapped at the precise moment the weapons were released. The intervalometer, a timing device for aerial cameras, along with camera mounts and mechanical triangular equipment were among Abrams's developments supplied to the military during World War II.

GORDON HALL

ARMY AIR CORPS PILOT

The people who knew Gordon E. Hall the best were not surprised that he soared up the ranks of the U.S. Army Air Corps. Like many young men, Hall was eager to serve his country as soon as he collected his diploma from Wapella High School in May 1935. But the seventeen-year-old was a few months shy of being old enough to join the ranks. Hall enrolled at the University of Illinois, studying commerce and business administration, while working to complete flight training at Chanute Air Base in nearby Rantoul.

Hall's friends waited anxiously for their eighteenth birthdays and the potential start of their commitment to the military. Among the hometown students influenced by Hall's decision to become a pilot was Ernest Thorp, who watched in amazement as Hall swooped low over the high school and the Halls' home, a sign to the pilot's parents that he was ready for a ride home from Chanute.

Hall was awarded his wings, along with a second lieutenant's commission, following advanced training in November 1940 at Gulf Coast Air Corps Training Center at Kelly Field, in Texas.

The Earthquakers

In July 1942, Hall and the other members of the 12th Bombardment Group left Fort Dix, New Jersey, for overseas duty. The B-25 bomb group, known as "The Earthquakers," was assigned missions in Northern Africa, Egypt and the Mediterranean.

Technical Sergeant Robert E. Wilson chronicled the group's experiences in *The Earthquakers: Overseas History of the 12th Bomb Group*. Written in frank "call a spade a spade" terms, Wilson's book is a firsthand account into what the group encountered.

Gordon Hall.

Near misses were recorded. The first came over Egypt in October 1942 when a German 88mm shell hit his plane in the squadron. The shell passed through the wing structure, leaving a gaping fourteen-inch hole but the crew intact. About one year later, Hall narrowly escaped death while flying as copilot with an Italian pilot in an SM-79 medium bomber. After receiving a few instructions, Hall took over as pilot on a second flight.

"Evidently there was some miscommunication as to who worked what, because the takeoff ended in a broken landing gear and a smash-up," Wilson wrote in his diary. Unable to break free of an Italian parachute, in the plane with one engine ablaze, Hall was rescued by the copilot. Hall flew close to fifty missions, including the group's first mission in Egypt in August 1943 against enemy airfields at Daba and Fuka and port facilities at Matruh. In a United Press story quoting the young operations officer from central Illinois, the raid was termed "a vicious dogfight." "One of the bombing squadrons in the all-American formation was led by Capt. Gordon E. Hall of Wapella, Ill. A tall blond, he claims to have the 'best gunner in the outfit'—Tech. Sgt. William T. Cross of Terrell, Texas. 'The gunner has the toughest job of them all,' Hall said. 'He has to keep the pilot posted on what's going on.'

The August 17, 1943 edition of *Stars and Stripes* recorded the 12th Bomb Group's first anniversary of overseas battle. By the time the group moved to Sicily, Hall was twenty-five and one of the youngest men to serve as a lieutenant colonel in the U.S. Army. Hall received four citations in 1943, including the Distinguished Flying Cross, the Oak Leaf and several clusters and the Silver Star. The 12th Bomb Group was recognized with a Distinguished Unit Citation for its actions during the North African campaign.

Back home in Wapella, Hall's parents, John and Erma, and his three sisters, Eleanor, Geraldine and Gloria, stayed busy as they waited for their son and brother to return home. John Hall worked for a water well company and later served as a Clinton police officer.

Erma Hall's new position at her brother's service station garnered headlines in an area newspaper. Hall's "blue-eyed vivacious mother is doing her bit on the home front by taking a man's place as Clinton's first and only woman filling station attendant," noted the July 1, 1943 *Daily Pantagraph* story. "This kind of work keeps me busy, and I don't have time to think of things....I'm sure proud of my boy," Mrs. Hall told a reporter.

But the family's worst fears were realized on October 1, 1943, when Lieutenant Colonel Gordon E. Hall was killed in what was described by high-ranking officer as a "freak accident" in a twin-engine German plane in Sicily. Wilson watched as the tragedy unfolded and later wrote this account:

> *On October 1st, the 12th Bombardment Group suffered their biggest loss to date overseas. Lt. Col. Gordon Hall, Operations Officer of the Group, had located a Me 210 and had it repaired. Impatient to go up in this plane, the Colonel decided on the 1st to take off just before dinner. At 1130 hours he taxied on the runway and opened the throttles. No one will ever know for sure what happened, but one engine ran away, the plane veered to the left though it kept rolling and finally raised off the ground. About this time the plane left the ground, the nose cannon fired a couple of shots. Why this happened was a mystery. When I saw the Colonel, he was clear of the ground and just leaving the landing area. Immediately after he left the field plateau, he soared possibly a 100 feet high. He went into a vertical bank to the left and dived into the ground. The plane exploded and caught fire immediately. For nearly an hour, the fire raged. Cannon shells and ammunition exploded every few seconds.*

Hall's body had been somewhat protected from the fiery crash by tires that had fallen on top of him, Wilson wrote. His watch and wallet were recovered. Hall's body was escorted to the base at Ponte Olivio the next day by a formation of three B-25 Mitchells. "The death of Lt. Colonel Hall was certainly a shock to us. It had all happened so fast it was difficult for us to realize it," Wilson recalled. News of Hall's death was delivered to his family in a handwritten telegram.

THE SEARCH FOR ANSWERS

In a November 2, 1943 letter confirming the telegram message, Major General J.A. Ulio informed the parents that initial casualty reports indicated their son "was killed in an airplane crash." The army official promised more details when and if they became available.

As the community and family prepared for Hall's funeral at the Wapella Christian Church, the unanswered questions surrounding the crash added to everyone's grief. Erma Hall continued to search for answers, and twenty-three years after the loss of her son, Brigadier General William A. Wilcox provided insight into what had happened on the hillside in Sicily.

"For reasons that are unknown, Gordon's aircraft lost power almost as soon as it became airborne—and at the same time, he was over the end of the runway," the officer wrote in his letter to Hall's mother. The crash he was in was unavoidable, but Hall's one last act "of extreme presence of mind" kept others from becoming casualties.

"I must now explain that the major portion of our encampment was nestled against a hill, and the runway was on top of the hill. If Gordon had continued to glide, straight ahead from the end of the runway to his crash, he would have certainly plowed through many of the tents of the camp and killed many others with him....This he did not do. He kept his head and steered the plane sharply to the left and thus saved many who otherwise would have been victimized. He selected the isolated area and drove his plane to that spot for the crash," wrote the air force general. The operations officer "was a true flier, and I don't think he could have wished for himself a more fitting end," added Wilcox.

The general's opinion that Hall deliberately steered the plane away from his comrades dampened a suspicion that the plane had been booby-trapped by Germans, a practice used by the enemy to harm and deter Allied troops from recovering downed aircraft.

Hall and a second soldier killed overseas, Private Richard Evey of Clinton, were honored in 1945 when the Clinton Veterans of Foreign Wars post was named for the two fallen soldiers. Hall's body was returned to Illinois, where he was laid to rest at Woodlawn Cemetery in Clinton.

A postscript to Hall's story was discovered in the January 1999 issue of *Flying* magazine. Hall's longtime friend Ernest Thorp, another World War II veteran who was held as a prisoner of war, noticed Hall's name in an interview with army photographer Howard Levy.

Levy "got off one shot as the bomber went howling past toward its, and its pilot's, explosive destruction moments later," according to the photographer's account.

Diana Douglas, wife of Hall's nephew Gordon Douglas, tracked down Levy in 2000 in hopes that the final photo of Hall could be located. With Levy's help, the family secured a photo of the pilot in the Me 410 shortly before takeoff, but the final image was never found.

Hall's legacy is preserved in several large binders filled with flight records, photos, letters and souvenirs kept for decades by his parents and sisters and organized by Diana Douglas. In a final thought written by Douglas as part of Hall's biography, she recalled Ernest Thorp's opinion that Hall had the makings of a general, adding, "We'll never know."

The country lost "a pretty special person, even a hero," Douglas wrote. The photos and other mementos lovingly saved by the pilot's family for decades would have to tell his story. "Until now, Colonel Hall and his activities have been pretty much taken for granted. It's too bad that our family, as well as future generations, have to get 'acquainted' with him through photos and articles. Fascinating—the adventures he lived and the stories he could have told."

DONNA ANDERSON GROSS

PILOT, WASP CANDIDATE

As DeWitt County's youngest aviatrix, Donna Mae Anderson ascended the limits of aviation for female pilots before her dream of becoming a commercial flyer was cut short by the winds of politics and gender discrimination.

Anderson's passion for flying was fueled by the planes she watched on air strips within view of her home near Midland City, a town that amounted to a cluster of houses on the border between DeWitt and Logan Counties.

"Mom was kind of a tomboy. We always knew she flew a plane, and she was an expert with a rifle. She once won a dog in a hunting competition against men," recalled Diana Gross Battiste, the pilot's daughter.

By fourteen, she was learning to fly a plane, and by seventeen, she was garnering media attention as "DeWitt County's first and only aviatrix" after she earned her student pilot license. Part ownership in a plane owned by the Clinton Flying Club and a job as assistant manager at the Decatur Airport were among her accomplishments as a teen. She also was a member of the Civil Air Patrol.

Donna Anderson's high school yearbook photo.

Dreams Deferred

But Anderson, later known as Donna Anderson Gross, considered the airport post a steppingstone to her career as a commercial pilot. The unavailability of flying schools and small airports that were training men for the armed forces seemed to close the door for military flight training.

Undaunted, Anderson Gross anxiously awaited her eighteenth birthday—the age she could legally apply for a position with the Women Air Force Service Pilots (WASP), a group initially used to ferry army air force trainers to their destinations and light aircraft from the factories. The female pilots later delivered fighters and bombers as well.

Anderson Gross also spent the time working at a factory in Illiopolis near Decatur that manufactured small artillery shells.

On June 6, 1944, while living in Decatur, Anderson Gross received her acceptance letter for the Women's Flying Training program in Sweetwater, Texas. She was instructed to bring her pilot's logbook and certification for admission. The training at Avenger Field was thirty weeks and 210 hours of flying.

The salary for the Civil Service position was $150 per month during training and $250 monthly as a utility pilot—if she passed the course. Transportation costs to the air base—and back home if a trainee washed out—were paid by the pilot. Expenses for "subsistence and maintenance during training" were paid by students. The cost of room and board was estimated at $1.65 per day.

The handbook for trainees cautioned that "you are entering upon a phase of your life which will be so changed and so different from that to which you have been accustomed, that it will seem to be a new existence altogether." Famed female pilot Jacqueline Cochran was hired to lead the initiative to use the talents of female flyers as part of the war effort. Hundreds of women enrolled in the program the first two years.

Once a Pilot, Always a Pilot

Donna Mae Anderson's dream of flying for the military was disrupted after she and hundreds of other young female pilots found themselves in the crosshairs of a political debate over whether women should serve in the military. A proposal to militarize the WASPs was met with strong opposition

Donna Anderson's Civil Air Patrol certificate.

from some male aviators and members of Congress, along with influential members of the media.

In a series of e-mails she penned to her children shortly before her death in 2001, the disappointment remained palpable. "I finally reached the old age of 18 and was called to report to the WASPs. Had a big farewell party at the plant and went home to pack my bags for Waco, TX. I was to leave Saturday at 6:00 p.m. My Dad came home with the telegram that told me my class was canceled and there would be no further classes. Seems Ms. Cochran wanted us admitted to the armed services and the Senate wouldn't allow it."

The young aviatrix knew the breadth of her abilities and the loss the military suffered by denying admittance to her and other experienced flyers. "I had to go to Chanute Air Field for written and physical training. The exam was the same as they gave commissioned officers and I passed. So had I been a man, I would have at least been a lieutenant," she wrote. The contributions of female pilots were well documented during the two years they were allowed to assist the military.

"They fly the equivalent of more than seven times around the earth every day and pilot planes of many types and capabilities, from trainers up through the Thunderbolt, Mustang, Marauder and Fortress," the *New York Times* noted in a March 1944 article on the issue.

Advocates for women pilots rallied support and attempted to push through legislation that would allow the program to remain open. Anderson Gross and others whose careers were derailed by politicians received letters from women in Washington, D.C., urging them to fight on. Letters to lawmakers and newspapers followed.

"It became a matter of men's rights vs. women's rights and the male pilots being effectively organized were able to prevail with Congress at your direct expense," wrote two advocates in a letter to the DeWitt County student. The WASP program received more 25,000 applications, with 1,830 accepted. Graduates numbered 1,074 and 900 remained when the program ended. After the program was disbanded, many WASPs who wanted to continue to fly were rejected by commercial airlines fearing a negative backlash of public sentiment. In 1949, the U.S. Air Force offered commissions to former WASPs, but it did not include the ability to fly for the military. Women first entered air force pilot training in 1976 and fighter pilot training in 1993. Today, the air force has 960 female pilots, and 417 women serve as navigators.

After several weeks of unsuccessful lobbying of lawmakers, Anderson Gross went back to work at the Garfield Division of Houdaille-Hershey in Decatur, where she served as a secretary to the plant manager. She later moved with the company to Detroit, where she met her husband, Don Gross, and they started a family, including daughter Diana and son Don.

The family returned to Kenney in 1966 to live on the Anderson homestead. Anderson Gross worked as a secretary for the Clinton law firm of Herrick, Rudasill and Moss. Her skill and knowledge of aviation never waned.

After watching the landings by her neighbor John Warner at Hooterville Airport near Hallsville, she offered him some advice. "I stopped and watched your landings. If you'll slow your approach and pitch the nose up a little more when you touch down, your landings are going to be a lot of better," Warner recalled her telling him. It was clear to Warner that he was getting good advice. "I realized, 'You know what you're talking about.'"

In conversation with her children, Anderson Gross shared the single contribution she felt she had made during the war effort. It came during her time at the Garfield plant. "Our secret was revealed when the U.S. dropped the atomic bomb on Japan, and the war was over. We made a small little part of the bomb but received the Army-Navy E Award and a big celebration."

KARL M. BRENNAN

ARMY AIR CORPS MECHANIC

Karl M. Brennan was living in the small town of Lane, six miles east of Clinton, when he joined the U.S. Army Air Corps in December 1941. Brennan was stationed at Santa Maria Air Base in California after basic training. He was trained as a tail gunner, specializing in aviation mechanics and the P-38 twin-engine fighter plane.

Brennan in the cockpit of a Lockheed P-38 Lightning.

A certification as a master mechanic kept Brennan stateside for the duration of the war. He was transferred to nearly every air base in the continental United States, including Langley, Virginia, and bases in Texas, Colorado and Arizona. He was disappointed that the round of assignments did not include Chanute Air Base in Rantoul, the airfield closest to his home.

Every person fortunate enough to serve in a military aviation program has a favorite memory of their time working around pilots and planes. For Brennan, that moment came at Kessler Field in Mississippi when he had the chance to meet maverick aviator Major Greg "Pappy" Boyington, commander of the "Black Sheep" fighter squadron. Three decades after Boyington was shot down into the Pacific Ocean, his squadron's story would inspire the television series *Baa Baa Black Sheep*.

Brennan was discharged from the military in 1946 and returned to DeWitt County. The mechanical skills gained during his military service were put to good use during his thirty-five years with the Illinois Central Railroad.

WILLIAM BRYAN SMITH

RADIO OPERATOR

The bustling campus of the University of Illinois was filled with experiences unfamiliar to Bill Smith when he joined the 1942 freshmen class with his sights set on becoming a lawyer. But Smith's adjustment from small-town life in Clinton to college life was cut short after a few months when he was called to military service.

"They cleared out the university of men," Smith recalled years later to his wife. Smith joined the Army Air Corps and trained as a radio operator. A typical day for a recruit started with three hours of lectures, followed by hours building a radio receiver from scratch and several hours learning Morse code until eighteen words per minute could be successfully transmitted.

William Smith.

Heavy responsibility rested on the shoulders of radio operators. As a monitor of the combat cargo group's frequencies for any changes to the flight plan, the radio operator's skill enabled the pilot to communicate with other planes. The radio operators also maintained detailed logs of each mission.

Few assignments during the war required more astute technical skill than the cargo missions from India to China over the eastern end of the Himalayan Mountains. Known as "The Hump," the area was treacherous for pilots and their crews.

Bill Smith poses in front of a Bell P-39 Airacobra.

Asked to describe his work for his granddaughter's school assignment on the war, Smith wrote, "Our mission during the war was to supply the British Army whose duty was to drive the Japanese Army out of Burma. We carried supplies to the British Army and hauled back wounded British soldiers from Burma to hospitals in India. I flew 473 combat missions from India into Burma, and later from Burma into China across the Himalayan Mountains."

The yellowed pages of Smith's logbook chronicle the missions over the mountainous airspace, where life-threatening weather was the norm. Also expected by crews was the sight of downed aircraft in the gorges below the transport planes.

By the time the hauling ended in 1945, 776,532 tons of war materials had been flown to China over six routes ranging from twelve thousand to twenty thousand feet in altitude. More than 500 planes and 910 crew members, along with 130 passengers, were lost during the Hump operation.

Smith credited the pilots of the C-46 planes with bringing him home safely. After he was discharged, Staff Sergeant Smith returned to the University of Illinois and received his law degree in 1952 from the Lincoln College of Law in Springfield. He was a practicing attorney in his family's law firm for forty-seven years.

THE RICHARD QUINTON FAMILY

A FAMILY OF FLYERS

Richard and Mary Alice Quinton raised corn, soybeans and a crop of young aviators on the McLean County farm southwest of Heyworth that was home to three generations of Quintons before them.

As a child growing up on the 1,200-acre dairy and grain farm, Quinton shared a fascination of flying with his classmates at the Short Point School. Lessons were routinely paused when the sound of a biplane over the schoolhouse caught the attention of Ruth Sutter, the young schoolmarm, whose beau at the time was barnstormer Red Irwin. The residents of Heyworth and surrounding towns were familiar with Irwin's habit of buzzing over the landscape, barely missing every chimney in his path. Quinton's brother Bill, sister Eleanor and four girl cousins ran outdoors, their gaze fixed on the sky and Red's performance in the marvelous and mysterious new invention people called an "airplane."

"Dad was pretty excited. Red's excitement sparked a huge feeling inside Dad, a feeling that went real deep," Jim Quinton, one of the Quinton's six children, said of his father's childhood experience.

For Quinton, the desire to fly was one of the solid lines on the blueprint he mapped out as a young man. In his autobiography, Quinton recalled the spring of 1940, his senior year of high school. "I picked up a new library book our English teacher, Grace Karl, had ordered. It was entitled, 'I Wanted Wings,' written by Mr. Bierne Laye Jr., a military pilot. Once I opened the book and started reading, I couldn't put it down!"

Quinton's plan called for his acceptance into the U.S. Army Air Corps, where he would complete cadet flying school, earn his silver pilot's wings and leave as a second lieutenant. After his first year at Illinois State Normal University, he was anxious to have his sophomore year behind him, a milestone that would allow him to apply for cadet training.

Richard Quinton in front of his Boeing B-17 Flying Fortress.

The attack on Pearl Harbor near the end of his third semester stoked Quinton's resolve to join the military. A new offer from the Army Air Corps allowed aspiring flyers admission if they could pass a battery of exams. Quinton earned passing marks, but he faced another hurdle: his father's attitude toward flying had soured after a fatal plane crash in Bloomington struck too close to home. The parental permission for nineteen-year-old Quinton to join the air corps in December 1942 came from his mother. Following basic training in Fresno, California, Quinton began preflight training in Santa Ana, California.

In October 1943, he moved on to Ryan Field in Tucson, Arizona, where he made his first solo flight. Slow rolls, loops, stalls and lazy eights were a few of the maneuvers he mastered. Quinton's experience piloting B-17s came with his relocation to Biggs Field in Texas and an intense schedule of six-hour training missions as part of Combat Crew 8227. The regimen prepared him for his assignment with the 8th Air Force in Deopham Green, England, the same base his friend Ernest Thorp was stationed before his capture by the Germans.

In his letters home from overseas, Quinton described a demanding flight schedule, sometimes lasting fifteen hours straight. Quinton was awarded five Air Medals and five Battle Stars for his thirty-five combat missions over Germany. Recognition of his lifesaving efforts on behalf of a gunner on one of those missions would come as a surprise—nearly five decades later.

While on leave on August 6, 1945, a new bulletin delivered over the radio shocked Quinton and the world as he milked cows on the family farm. An American B-29 bomber had dropped an atomic bomb over the Japanese city of Hiroshima. Jim Quinton recalled his father's reaction to the bombings: "It was so out of the realm of possibility for people. They just could not believe it."

Four months after a second atomic bomb exploded over Nagasaki, Quinton was discharged from the service. In June 1946, he married his college sweetheart, Mary Alice Glenn, a future home economics teacher. The couple moved to Michigan, where he received a degree in animal science.

His love of aviation remained strong as ever. "Dad thought it was fun to hang around the airports, and he was always hungry to try and do new things," said Jim Quinton.

Quinton's appetite for flying was satisfied again in 1954 when he and his younger brother Bill managed to buy an Ercoup. Their enjoyment was short-lived. A storm heavily damaged the plane, leaving it beyond repair and forcing them to scrape more money together, this time for a Taylorcraft Model B with a price tag of $300. The two-seater "tail dragger" took practice and skill to fly. Takeoffs could be tough to navigate in the plane with the third wheel located under the rudder. "The hardest thing about it wasn't in the air but on the ground. You can only see through the left and right windows until you're in the air, level. Then you can see through the front window," explained Jim Quinton.

The bargain aircraft also needed new fabric over its wings and fuselage, a process completed over the winter in a hangar at Logan County Airport. With profits from the sale of the renovated Taylorcraft, the brothers bought a Piper Super Cruiser, a larger plane with a more powerful engine. In 1958, the Quintons packed up their family for Richard's new job as a farm advisor in Arizona's Yuma County. Ranchers in the area were pleased to have an experienced pilot who could fly them around the Southwest.

When the Quintons returned to the Heyworth farm about five years later, the purchase of another plane—this one a J-3 Piper Cub—was on the horizon. Jim Quinton learned to fly the plane, another "tail dragger," without lights or radar. His siblings Jay, John, Joyce and Jerry also earned their pilot's licenses. Their sister Janice did not take up flying. The elder Quinton "was proud as punch all the time that his kids learned to fly," said Jim Quinton.

Aviation also played a role in the Quintons' farming operation. Planes ferried Quinton to pick up parts from dealers as far away as the Quad Cities in northwest Illinois. He joined other pilots from the area in social gatherings at Red Irwin's former landing strip, the Hooterville Airport south of Hallsville, hosted by the airport's new owner, John Warner.

The Quinton brothers and a third partner bought a Cessna 172 in 1970. Jim Quinton sometimes used the plane to survey crops as part of his work with the Chicago Board of Trade, an arrangement that gained the approval of his father because it boosted the balance in his father's "airplane fund."

On Memorial Day 1975, Quinton stretched the boundaries of aviation and farming by planting a crop of soybeans by air. Using a modified crop dusting plane, he seeded two bushels per acre of beans onto twenty-two acres of wheat. "We soaked the beans in milk cans then dumped the swollen beans into the plane's hopper. The crop duster flew low and slow as he could in his biplane," said Jim Quinton. The beans grew vigorously under the wheat canopy and stood about a foot tall on July 3 when the wheat was harvested. When the yield of thirty bushels per acre of soybeans was added to the sixty bushels of wheat, the experiment netted more income than a single corn crop. The air seeding was deemed a success.

For the Quinton offspring, having an aircraft on the farm was as common as the tractors parked in the machine shed. "It might just be flying around for 30 minutes, looking over everybody's back fence. Our Dad didn't go bowling or go to coffee shops or the other places the neighbors went. He had airplanes," said Jim Quinton. Jay Quinton made a career of aviation. After his graduation from the Air Force Academy, Captain Quinton logged thousands of hours flying C-130s. His experience flying multi-engine jets over open water made him a desirable candidate for a commercial airline position carrying passengers to Europe. Northwest Airlines hired Quinton as pilot after his 1995 retirement from the military.

Jim Quinton's career managing grain elevators allowed him to fly to locations in several midwestern states. But the increased costs associated with aviation has put private plane ownership out of reach for most people, Quinton said. "Dad owned planes from the 1950s when it was possible for the value of the various aircraft to gain in value while they were owned so their equity built up and up with each upgrade. Now, unless it's part of what you're doing, it's almost prohibitive as an indulgence," he said.

The Flying Farmers was an organization that once boasted more than eleven thousand members, included the Quintons. Land It, a program for the wives of aviator-farmers, was established by Mary Alice Quinton. The motivation behind the Flying Farmers program was "to at least train them enough to be able to land in an emergency. Mom was kind of a nervous pilot but she did it to help him." The women were given ten hours of instruction.

Forty-eight years after Quinton returned home, he received a long-overdue Distinguished Flying Cross for his act of heroism on February 23, 1945.

The flying Quintons: Richard with sons Jay, Jonathan, Jerry and Jim. *Front row*: Joyce, flight instructor Vinny White and Mary Alice Quinton.

As copilot on the B-17 flying at twenty-five thousand feet in a sixty-below temperature, Quinton was tasked with checking the oxygen connections of the ten-member crew. When turret gunner Sergeant Robert Glaeser did not respond to the intercom call, Quinton left his seat to check on him. He found the turret rotating and Glaeser weak and purple from lack of oxygen.

Quinton and navigator Lieutenant Roy Metcalf moved Glaeser to a heated body bag in the nose section of the aircraft. After several hours on oxygen, he recovered. Crew members submitted details of the incident to the air force, and the medal and plaque arrived from Andrews Air Force Base. "That was just part of the whole ballgame," Quinton, then seventy, told a reporter after the medal arrived.

In his final aviation purchase, Quinton traded the Cessna-172 for a Mooney Statesman, a plane with a cruising speed of around 185 miles per hour. At the time he retired from farming and flying in 1985, Richard Quinton owned three planes.

The lifetime of flying was part of Quinton's blueprint of "central core principles," according to his son. "That was his dream, from the time he was a farm boy growing up in Heyworth."

WILLIAM C. CALVIN

B-17 BOMBER PILOT

On November 1, 1943, the four B-17 groups of the 5th Bomb Wing and two B-24 units of the 9th Air Force were combined with two fighter groups from the 12th Air Force to form the new 15th Air Force, the strategic air force in the Mediterranean. The first commander was General Jimmy Doolittle. On November 2, 1943, the 15th opened for business when it bombed the Rimini Marshaling yard in northern Italy.

In December 1943, all of the B-17 Flying Fortress groups moved from North Africa to Italy. Midwesterner William C. Calvin, a major and aircraft commander in the 15th, piloted one of the B-17 bombers. In a series of interviews with a local columnist years later, Calvin recalled his experiences. "Four, four, forty-four," Calvin said thoughtfully, referring to the calendar date of April 4, 1944. "That's the day I saw a jet airplane for the very first time."

"We were operating out of Italy," Calvin began, "and on that day we were on our way home from Munich. During the briefing session they told us that this was going to be a milk run, a real cabbage patch run. And it was, too. We didn't encounter enemy fighters and the anti-aircraft fire, flak, was light. We had dropped our load and were on our way home, still flying a good formation."

Calvin, who later became a judge, described formation flying. "In a multi-engine aircraft, the copilot is just that: a second pilot in the cockpit. My copilot and I shared the workload. During formation flying we would alternate jobs every 15 minutes. One of us would fly the aircraft and hold

Bill Calvin.

our position in the formation while the other would monitor the flight and engine instruments and operate the throttles as necessary. Formation flying is precision work and it is tiring. Fifteen minutes at a time is about enough."

He continued, "It takes a long time to come down from 30,000 feet, so, not long after leaving a target, we would begin our descent. We would fly 'downhill' all the way back to our base in Italy—coming down at 500 feet per minute—just a long, slow descent with a let-down over the airfield at the end.…My copilot and I had the ship trimmed for descent and we were taking turns flying formation. Back and forth, all the way home."

This long, slow descent was primarily employed for fuel management. Each of the B-17 bomber's Wright 1820 radial engines developed 1200 horsepower and burned 60 gallons of high-octane aviation fuel per hour. Burning fuel at the combined rate of about 250 gallons per hour, the B-17 bomber consumed most of its fuel load while climbing to altitude and reaching the target.

"Many times, we were over our target with our fuel tanks reading only one-fourth full," Calvin recalled. "Many times. With that long slow descent we could still make it all the way back home. Many times, we landed with the needles on our fuel gauges hovering just above empty.…We were down to about 25,000 feet when all of a sudden my tail gunner got on the interphone." The interphone is the aircraft intercom, the way for pilot and crews to talk within the aircraft. The men were trained to speak clearly and calmly and to convey their messages precisely. Yelling and swearing over the interphone were strictly verboten.

"Major, six o'clock, high. Inbound, fast. Don't recognize that wing profile," reported Calvin's tail gunner.

"Naturally, that gets you excited," Calvin continued. "So I said, 'Throw some tracers at him and let's see what he does.'"

"Of course, when you are up front in an aircraft and you hear the sound of guns firing from the tail, you aren't sure whether it's your bullets going out or the other fellow's bullets coming in. The pilot and copilot seats were armor plated and I kind of scrunched down in my seat, trying to get as much of me behind the armor plate as possible, just in case. Actually, it was my tail gunner firing, but I wasn't certain.…Ours was a very good crew. But at

Calvin poses in front of a Boeing Stearman Model 75 trainer biplane.

about that point my top turret gunner broke in on the interphone, yelling and swearing, 'He's moving so fast I can't get my guns on him!'"

In aerial combat, speaking calmly and concisely is often easier said than done. "At that moment the German ship dove through our formation, just off my left wingtip. He came through at about 75 degrees nose low, traveling fast."

"I can still see that aircraft," recalled Calvin. "Some kind of fighter, mottled gray, cigar shaped fuselage, black German crosses on the tail. As I looked out to my left, the German pilot looked out to his right. He looked at me and I looked at him, and our eyes met. And then he was gone.…Our interphone was busy then, with everyone asking, basically, 'What the heck was THAT?'"

"We found out later that it was a German Messerschmitt 262, a single seat jet fighter with a turbine engine under each wing. The Me 262 was the first operational jet of the war, anywhere in the world.…Our B-17 cruised at an indicated airspeed of about 165 mph, fully loaded. Empty, it cruised a little faster, around 175 to 185 mph. It had a maximum airspeed of 250 mph. But that was with all four engines at full power, or 'combat emergency' as they called it, and we never really operated that fast."

He continued, "The Me 262, on the other hand, cruised at something like 300–350 mph. In other words, it had practically a 2 to 1 speed advantage over us.…No sooner had the German gone through when two silver P-51

Mustangs tore through right after him, right on his tail. The German had such a speed advantage over everything that the only way a propeller-driven aircraft had even the slightest chance of catching him was in a high-speed, straight-down dive. Those Mustangs could do it....They could handle the stress of that kind of maneuver."

"They chased him down from 25,000 feet," Calvin remembered, "almost all the way to the ground....In fact, that really became our fighters' tactic against jets. The Me 262 had a short fuel range. They would climb to our altitude, make a couple of passes at us, and then dive for the deck, low on fuel. Once they were down low, they would throttle back and run for home. Skimming over the treetops at 300 mph made them a very hard target to hit. But if our fighters could stay with them during the dive and catch them or overtake them in their round-out at the bottom, they had a pretty good chance of shooting them down."

"We never did learn what happened to that jet. But if Hitler had gotten them into the air sooner, well, the outcome of the war might have been a lot different....I know I'll never forget that day in April, 1944," Calvin concluded. "I was there for the dawn of the jet age."

Tuskegee Airmen

"On one mission to Frankfurt, Germany," Calvin recalled, "our ship was in about the middle of the lead formation of the groups on the way to the target that day. Friendly aircraft were stacked above us and below us and staggered behind us. We had just crossed over into enemy territory....Once we had entered enemy territory, once we knew we were in enemy airspace, aircrews were allowed to 'clear' their guns, to test fire them with a short burst. It was standard operating procedure to do this."

Calvin added, "All the planes in our group test fired their guns at about the same time. We could hear their gunfire above us, below us and all around us....One of our engines began running rough and then, with no warning, it shut down altogether. When we couldn't get it re-started, we had to feather the propeller and kept going on just three engines." When a multi-engine airplane loses an engine, you can maintain altitude or you can maintain airspeed, but you can't maintain both."

"All of our training and experience emphasized the importance of 'group integrity,'" he continued. "A B-17 bomb group was put together in such a way that the aircraft in a formation defended each other with overlapping fields of fire. An aircraft crew wasn't just defending their own ship; they were helping to defend every other ship around them.... That combined fire power was massive, and it could be deadly. If I were a German fighter pilot, I wouldn't want to face it....We elected to stay with our group for as long as we could."

He continued, "So, first, we lightened the aircraft by 'pickling' our load—just opening our bomb bay doors and dropping our bombs, regardless. We could do that because we were over enemy-held territory. We dropped our bombs several miles before we reached our target at Frankfurt, but at least they hit something held by the enemy."

"Whenever a heavy bomber drops its load," Calvin noted, "the aircraft surges in the air when it sheds all that extra weight. It jumps up at least 20 feet. Getting rid of the load enabled us to stay with our group. We made the bomb run in formation and turned for home with the rest of our group. But after that, we couldn't keep up."

"All the way back home we kept drifting back. We drifted from the front of our group into the rear of our group. Then we fell behind them and began drifting back into the lead of the group following us. Over the next hour or so we drifted back through that second group, too. We finally fell behind them, too....All the while the crew was throwing out anything that wasn't bolted down," Calvin recalled. "We did everything we could think of to lighten the ship. We threw our life vests and life rafts overboard. We threw out empty oxygen bottles."

"But we just couldn't keep up. We kept drifting back....We drifted back through the second group and into the third group. After we got out of enemy airspace, we even threw out our extra belts of ammunition. Several of the crew threw their guns overboard."

He continued, "Finally, we were way out behind everyone, all by ourselves, with no way to defend ourselves if anything else went wrong. The radio operator dialed up the emergency channel and I got on the radio and said, 'I need fighter cover and I need it right now!'"

"I had no more than made that transmission when a southern accent drawled back over the radio, 'Look up here, white boy!'"

Above Calvin's stricken bomber flew a silver P-51 Mustang with distinctive, red-painted tail surfaces. The Mustang pilot had already seen the struggling bomber and come to the rescue of Calvin's crew. He flew above and ahead of Calvin, circling in a broad arc, looking for trouble. "I've never been so glad to see fighter support in my entire life," Calvin remarked.

Bomber crews of the 15th Air Force knew the four squadrons of 332nd Fighter Group—the 99th, 100th, 301st and 302nd—as "Red Tail Angels." Flying P-51 Mustangs with distinctive red tails, by war's end the 332nd was credited with damaging or destroying more than four hundred enemy aircraft and never losing any of the B-17 Flying Fortresses that they escorted on missions over Europe.

The P-51 pilots were all Black, graduates of the Army Air Forces Flying Training Program at Tuskegee, Alabama. The air corps had reluctantly admitted the first Black aviation cadets in 1941. The outfits remained segregated throughout the war.

The 332nd was led by Lieutenant Colonel Benjamin O. Davis Jr., the first Black officer to earn pilot's wings in the U.S. Army Air Force. A gifted flyer, Davis was a stern taskmaster who demanded the best from his men. "There was constantly before us the challenge," Davis wrote many years after the war, "to refute the widely accepted belief that blacks could not learn to fly airplanes or participate successfully in combat operations." The red-tailed P-51 escorted Calvin's bomber all the way back to Italy. When Calvin and his copilot had their home field in sight, the P-51 pilot waggled his wings in farewell, peeled off and headed for home. "Those guys were superb pilots," Calvin said of the Tuskegee airmen, "and absolutely dedicated to their work."

"There's a postscript to my story, too," said Calvin. "After we got back to our base, the mechanics had to tear down our bad engine to see what was wrong. They found a spent .50-caliber shell casing in the induction system. Whether it was one of our own shells from when we cleared our guns, or whether it was a shell casing from another aircraft, we never did know. But that's what caused our engine to fail—one of our very own shells."

WILLIAM P. HARROLD

U.S. AIR FORCE FLIGHT ENGINEER

For William P. Harrold, of Clinton, Illinois, aviation opened the door into an entirely new world. "I was drafted on January 15, 1943," Bill Harrold recalled in conversations with pilot John Warner. "I didn't have any interest in aviation when I got drafted, but it was something I got into, and felt fortunate that I did, once I got started."

"When we went through induction at Belleville, Illinois, they had two train coaches and they called out names. They said, 'This bunch goes to this coach, and that bunch goes to that coach. This bunch went to the infantry,'" Harrold remembered. "And I was lucky enough to be called to the coach that went to the Army Air Force. In those days, the air force wasn't an independent branch of the service. It was still a part of the army."

"Of course, you have your basic training. When I first went in, they gave you aptitude tests as far as seeing if you'd be good in radio, you know, being a radio man on a plane, or if you'd be better in mechanics or something. I wasn't too good in radio. So I became a mechanic."

Harrold continued, "They sent us to the Curtiss Wright Technical Institute, a training base just outside of Glendale, California. We learned how to patch the fabric on planes and the mechanical details—the engine parts and components. It was school in California, and we learned about engines, aircraft structure, aircraft hydraulics and so forth. The training was really interesting. I really enjoyed it."

The Curtiss-Wright Technical Institute, established in 1929, was a trade school operated by Curtiss-Wright Corporation for aircraft maintenance training. Prior to World War II, it was one of three schools selected by the government to establish a civilian pilot training program. During the war, the institute trained more than 7,500 mechanics.

Harrold remembered, "Of course, we were stationed at an airbase in California. On the other end of the base was a squadron of Lockheed P-38 Lightnings, and those fellows used to take us up for a ride once in a while. They'd take out some of the radio equipment and make just enough room to haul a passenger. You'd sit back up behind the pilot with your knees underneath your chin. And those pilots would go up there and do loops and barrel rolls and snap rolls. They'd even dogfight with each other....And you'd think, 'Boy, if I ever get back on the ground in one piece—this is nothing like a cargo plane!'"

The Lockheed P-38 Lightning is an American single-seat, twin-engine fighter that was employed in World War II. The P-38 incorporated a distinctive twin tail boom design with a central nacelle that carried the pilot. It was the most innovative plane of its day, combining the speed of two turbocharged engines with overwhelming firepower. It could climb at 3,300 feet per minute, and it flew one hundred miles per hour faster than any other aircraft in the world.

The Lightning was extremely forgiving in flight and could tolerate a pilot's poor handling. Because of the twin booms and large horizontal stabilizer, bailing out of a P-38 was tricky. To get out in an emergency, it was necessary for the pilot to jettison the canopy, roll the aircraft onto its back and drop out while the ship was upside down.

The German fighter pilots called the P-38 Lightning the "fork-tailed devil."

Ferrying Command

"I started out as a line mechanic, pulling inspections and doing repair work and such," said Harrold. His mechanical ability and obvious enthusiasm for aviation brought an opportunity his way. "This older master sergeant that was over me said, 'We're going to put you on flying status.' And I said, 'You're not.' He insisted and I said, 'I don't think I'd like it.' He tried to convince me otherwise. 'You don't have to work as hard, and you get half your base pay in flight pay. You'll really like it. I'm gonna set it up.'"

When Harrold was posted to active flight status, he was assigned to the Air Transport Command (ATC), which was created during World War II and served as the airline of the U.S. military. The ATC delivered supplies and equipment from the United States to overseas combat theaters, ferried new aircraft from factories to operating airbases and provided airline-style transportation to military personnel.

"I was in the ferrying command when I was first into it. We were ferrying aircraft from the Ford plant at Willow Run, where they were making B-24 Liberators. And we ferried them to practically every state in the Union. Then we'd fly back on civilian airlines. These were brand-new aircraft." The Consolidated B-24 Liberator is an American four-engine heavy bomber designed by Consolidated Aircraft of San Diego, California. The Liberator had a very modern design when it was introduced in 1939, resulting in a high cruise speed, long range and the ability to carry a heavy load. Compared to other multi-engine heavy aircraft, the B-24 was difficult to fly and required constant attention at the controls.

Harrold told Warner, "We even had some women copilots. They weren't actually connected with the service. They were civilian employees. Some of them were just excellent pilots. Of course, you handle that B-24 and you're trying to bring it in on the tricycle landing gear and you've got that tail skid back there. Very few could bring it in on the nose wheel."

He continued, "As flight engineer on a B-24 I rode in a place behind the pilot. There wasn't a lot to do. Of course, they wanted you to keep track of fuel consumption and calculate what you'd use for so many hours of flight....When we were ferrying, you'd take a plane to a base, and then they'd send you back on the civilian airlines. And we had priority, even over a general if he was going to leave."

Harrold went on, "Like there was a pilot, copilot, engineer and radio operator. They stayed together. They wanted you back at the base as a team so they could send you out again as a team....When we were ferrying, it would be the same type of aircraft each time. We'd fly one B-24 and then we'd go back to pick up another B-24. They were all bare metal too. They were all shiny silver. And not only were they not painted, they didn't even have any insignia on them."

Stateside

Not only did Harrold fly as flight engineer on board new B-24s, but he also logged time in the C-54. These flights took him all over North America.

"As flight engineer on a C-54," he explained, "I had a lot to do. On takeoffs I held the throttles forward, and the pilot just guided the nose wheel. The copilot made the actual takeoff. If the pilot was coming in on final approach and needed something that he was too busy to do himself, he'd tell the flight engineer to give him full power or ten degrees of flaps or something like that."

"On the C-54, there was a jump seat that folded down between the pilot and copilot. After you got everything stabilized, there were two bunks back behind there, and it was always a fight to see who was going to get a bunk. But the pilot and copilot couldn't get out until I got out. So it was a fight between me and them and the radio operator," Harrold laughed. "I think it was in St. Louis or some airfield in Missouri, and we were using a short runway. It was a *short* runway. We were flying a C-54. We got clearance to get out to the end of the runway. Then the pilot set our brakes, like a parking brake in a car. I held the throttles until we showed a certain RPM reading on the engines. Those engines were just roaring, and you could feel the aircraft shaking with the strain. And when the pilot kicked that brake loose, we really surged. Of course, we had to, just to clear the fence. When we broke ground, it felt like that aircraft had just jumped into the air."

"I got into flying 'transition' where they were checking out a new pilot," Harrold continued. "There were black curtains in the cockpit so the pilot couldn't see outside. The engineer had to sit by a back window and watch for planes, and the radio operator sat by the other window to watch for planes because they couldn't see anything from up front. It was like being in a dark room. They were flying on instruments only. I never was very comfortable doing that work, but you had to take your turn. Everybody had so many hours that they had to put in."

He added, "I remember doing stalls in a C-47. We'd get plenty of altitude, and then the pilot would pull up the nose, like we were climbing. Then he'd pull up the nose even further, into a climb that was too steep for the aircraft to handle. Well, that would make the stall. The ship would shudder all over. When I looked out at the wings, they were flapping like the wings of a bird! Of course, about that time, the nose would drop over and we'd fly out of the stall. I never did like it much but it was something you had to do."

"One time we were flying into Quebec, and when we were taxiing we saw Winnie Churchill. He was going by in another airplane and was sitting right in the window with that cigar in his mouth."

Flying to India

"In the fall of 1944, the word came down that we were being transferred overseas. We were being stationed in India, and we were flying ourselves there," Harrold recalled. "We left the United States from Florida and flew to Puerto Rico. We were flying a Curtiss C-46 Commando. The C-46 had a lot of hydraulic problems. A lot of the controls would get so they wouldn't work on account of hydraulic leaks. I don't know why because they were built by Curtiss-Wright."

Created in 1929 from the consolidation of Curtiss, Wright and a variety of affiliated suppliers, the Curtiss-Wright Corporation immediately became the largest aircraft manufacturer in the nation. During World War II, the company manufactured more than 142,000 aircraft for the U.S. military.

Curtiss aircraft served around the globe in every theater of operation. From start to finish, the Curtiss C-46 Commando was a pain in the neck. The aircraft's hydraulic system—mechanics said it was a "plumber's nightmare"—required nearly constant inspection and repair. The electronic pitch control on the propellers was troublesome and plagued with defects; in-flight propeller failures were to be expected. With at least thirty-one known instances of in-flight fires or explosions, the C-46 was called the "flying coffin" by ATC pilots.

"We stopped in two places in South America, Belem and Natal," Harrold noted. "When we left Natal, you had to get out to the end of the runway and preflight your engines by running them up to operating speed and checking their performance, and then the gas truck would come out and top off your tanks. The tanks had to be completely filled to make the flight. And you had to wait until the wind was just right, too."

"We flew from Natal to the Ascension Islands, a long trip over water. From the Ascension Islands the crew flew another over-water route to Casablanca, in Morocco, then across the northern part of Africa and the Arabian Sea to Dhaka, India. Next stop: Tezgoan."

Flying the Hump

"Flying the Hump" is the nickname that pilots gave the cargo hauling operation that crossed the Himalayan Mountains into China during World War II. More than one thousand men and six hundred aircraft were lost over the six-hundred-mile route. The only way to supply China in its fight against Japan, the Hump was the toughest flying in the world.

The jet stream winds in the Himalayan Mountains tossed airplanes up to thirty thousand feet and, the next instant, shoved them down to six thousand feet. "When we first started flying 'the Hump,' the lowest we could get was twenty-three thousand feet. And then they found a pass where we could go through around sixteen thousand and seventeen thousand feet," Harrold remembered. "We would fly from India to China, get the plane emptied, and then fly back on basically the same route. When we were flying B-24s that had been converted to tankers, the fuel had to be pumped out and we had a longer wait before starting back. When we had the C-54s, the DC-4s, we hauled fifty-five-gallon drums—each load weighed around seventeen thousand pounds. The drums were on pallets, and they had forklifts to load them off and the Chinese to move them around, so we didn't even have to touch them. All you had to do was see that your plane was serviced right. I checked over the engines and so forth when I first got there, and then I'd do a lot of it all over again before we took off. You never knew when one of those people might do something."

The trip from India to China took five to seven hours, depending on conditions. Crew were assigned to aircraft they had been trained on. For Harrold, that meant B-24s that had been converted to tankers. "I think it was on my first or second flight over in a B-24, and I was green and scared. My pilot, a young second lieutenant, had put the aircraft on automatic pilot and was sitting up there reading a *True Romance* magazine. That's what he was reading, I swear!"

Things turned dangerous. "The wings started icing up, and he didn't even notice. Everybody was getting pretty anxious, and finally he tried to get the plane off automatic pilot and he couldn't get the deicers to break that ice on the wings. But finally he got it loose and we didn't lose too much altitude."

Harrold told Warner of another close call: "Once we were flying a C-54 around eighteen thousand feet and we lost the number one engine, and the feathering pump wouldn't work. We weren't even close to the mountains yet. The engine started running rough, and then it just went dead. When a propeller windmills, the vibration and stress can tear an engine right out of its mount. The pilot got concerned because he couldn't get the feathering pump to work. He couldn't hydraulically turn the propeller blades parallel to the airflow to stop their windmilling."

He continued, "So he sent the radio operator and me back to pull the hinge pins on the cargo doors and let them blow away. We were afraid that the doors might be swept back into the horizontal stabilizer on the tail. Then we had to roll the fuel barrels out the cargo opening. Of course, at that altitude, you had to wear an oxygen mask while trying to do all this. All the while the pilot was circling, losing altitude. We could see our barrels hit the little grass huts way down below, and we knew we were probably killing people. But we couldn't help it."

"We got rid of the weight of the fifty-five-gallon drums of fuel, and the pilot was able to maintain his altitude. And we turned around and went back to our base on three engines. When we got just about to our field, the feathering pump started to work again. But we still landed because we had the doors off the aircraft, and we didn't know how much damage we had done to the tail surfaces."

He recalled, "We just kept wondering, 'If we get these drums out, how much altitude will it give us?' He was a very good pilot, and I had all the faith in the world in him, but is still had us wondering."

Pilots fought icing, poor visibility, violent wind, violent storms, equipment failures, fatigue, inexperience, fear and the Japanese. "If the mountains don't get you," went the air crews' refrain, "the Japanese will….The Japanese were attacking some of our planes that were hauling gasoline. And all you had was a .45-caliber pistol on your side."

The aircrews knew that their chances of survival were slim. Crashing or bailing out in the mountains or parachuting into enemy-held territory offered little hope. "Once a month or so, you'd fly search and rescue. As I remember, you did this four or five hours at a time. You'd be looking for crashed aircraft in the mountains along the route. They'd have a crew member at every window, even up in the glass nose. Sometimes they even had cameras," Harrold recalled. "You know, the tail was always the only thing that we ever found intact. The wings, the engines and the fuselage forward were always destroyed or completely burned. Sometimes they could make out the aircraft number on the tail, and then they could specifically account for the missing plane."

"The route is easy to navigate," one pilot quipped, "you just follow the crash sites."

"Before I got there, if you went down over the jungle, the headhunters would kill you," Harrold stated. "But by the time I got there the army had worked out a deal: if the natives would bring the crew in alive, they'd get salt and army blankets as a reward. I knew one guy who had been down and rescued by the headhunters three times."

"I was very fortunate," Harrold said in conclusion. "I didn't get hurt, and I got my time served and I got back home. I really enjoyed flying, and I thought about staying in the air force. I thought about working for one of the airlines, too, because it was obvious that commercial aviation was really going to grow after the war ended. But I think I just got tired of being in the service, and I really wanted to go home."

ERNEST THORP

B-17 BOMBER PILOT

Every generation has its true heroes—those who raised their hands without hesitation and said "I'll go" in response to a nation in need, leaving loved ones behind as they faced unknown dangers far from home. Before they became heroes, soldiers lived in neighborhoods and, in the case of Ernest Thorp, on farms in the heartland.

Thorp's story as an Army Air Force pilot begins with his childhood admiration for aviator Charles Lindbergh, a man he considered his hero after the pilot's famous 1927 flight across the Atlantic.

The decision by Thorp's close friend Gordon Hall, another resident of the small town of Wapella, to become a military pilot also influenced Thorp. Before he was killed in a crash while flying a captured German aircraft in Italy, Hall flew B-25s, the plane Thorp hoped to fly when he joined the military.

In 1939, Thorp started college at Illinois State University (formerly Illinois State College) and two years later transferred to the University of Illinois, where he learned to fly. He enlisted in the Army Air Force in 1942 while still a student and completed the Reserve Officers' Training Corps (ROTC) program.

In March 1943, midway through his senior year, Thorp was given full credit to graduate by the university and left for basic training in Texas. His family would later receive his diploma while he was a prisoner of war. Thorp's determination to be a pilot diminished any fears of the dangers encountered by wartime aviators.

Ernest Thorp in 1943.

"That's one of the things that's kind of strange in a sense, but you were always going to be the mother's son that never got hit. In other words, they would get the other guys—not you....I didn't think it could happen to me or would happen to me," Thorp told an interviewer in a lengthy 2009 conversation for the Abraham Lincoln Presidential Library in Springfield.

Much of the account of Thorp's military service comes from a diary he kept throughout his forty months as a pilot, including the nine months he spent as a prisoner of war. *My Stretch in the Service* was widely shared by Thorp before his death in 2017 at the age of ninety-five. Following flight training in Oklahoma, Thorp was assigned to a B-17 crew as a copilot. His crew took off in May 1944 from a training facility in Sioux City, Iowa, for Deopham Green, England, as part of the 729th Squadron, 452nd Bomb Group.

In a diary entry written after a practice formation mission, Thorp recalled seeing a crash nearby. "Watched a British Lancaster circle the field, stall out and crash about a mile from where I was at. Exploded and burned. I don't know how many escaped. Combat is getting closer every hour. Seeing these planes land with their wounded and battle-damaged gave me a funny feeling deep inside that you just can't laugh off all that well."

During his missions over both occupied France and Germany, Thorp saw many planes go down along with their pilots and crews. He reflected on the consequences of the war in his journal. "Boy. On the bomb run, you get a funny feeling all those bomb bay doors open, knowing soon death and destruction will fall from the insides. It's just like watching a long fly ball hit way out, and you hold your breath until you see the results: a hit, an error, foul-out, et cetera," Thorp wrote after his fifteenth mission.

Thorp opened his diary on August 4, 1944, with a note: "This day began as a snafu right from the beginning." Upset that a paperwork error kept him from a scheduled trip to London on leave, Thorp was assigned a new, somewhat anxious crew on a plane that would take off in heavy fog.

Things would only get worse on his eighteenth mission. After the plane was hit multiple times by flak, Thorp took over the controls. With no hope of bringing the plane down safely and a noticeable fire over the left wing, Thorp made the decision to bail out over the North Sea.

Gunner Sergeant Beyer and Ernest Thorp.

After forty-five minutes of intense prayers in the cold water, a mast appeared, one of the fishing boats that had spotted the four-member crew. "I thought it was going to pass me up, but it eventually turned and headed my way. I shouted and tried to wave, and lo, the mast changed course and headed for me. It was a fishing boat and never a more welcome sight for a guy in my situation, though I knew the occupants would be Germans," Thorp wrote in his diary.

The fishermen picked up Thorp, along with his pilot, navigator and an engineer. They were given a shot of rum—a first for the nondrinking farmer—and wrapped in blankets. "We were now prisoners of war—no more missions for us."

Thorp spent the next nine months in a series of POW camps, starting with Dulag Luft and later Stalag Luft III in Sagan, shortly after the daring "Great Escape" in which seventy-seven Allied prisoners managed to tunnel their way of out of captivity. (Most were recaptured within days.)

In late January 1945, with Soviets approaching, Thorp and other prisoners were forced to march to Stalag Luft VII-A during the coldest German winter in living history. The POWs lacked food, clothing and medical care. At one point, the men were crammed into a boxcar—sixty POWs packed like sardines—for three days and three nights.

Thorp narrowly escaped being shot during the stay at Stalag VII-A "because I was trying to slice a piece off a board to burn, and here comes a general with a tommy gun and I ducked around a corner. He didn't chase me, fortunately, but I could have been shot for doing that because I was destroying Germany's property."

On April 29, 1945, a calm, peaceful Sunday morning, the POWs were getting ready for chapel outside the barracks when an American P-51 did a barrel roll over the barracks, setting off cheers. The sound of gunfire told them that American troops had to be close.

When the soldiers saw the American flag go up over the town of Moosburg, they knew that the news of their liberation was real. "That's when you see 100,000 men cry, cheer, pray—bedlam. Then the tanks come in, knocked down the gate and come parading down the corridor, covered with humanity. Everybody crawled on these tanks, POWs, just for the ride. And then we knew we were free men," Thorp recalled. After twelve days of medical care and rest, Thorp was on his way across the Atlantic, headed home after a harrowing time abroad. A steak dinner at Fort Dix in New Jersey came with a train ticket to Chicago, the final stretch of Thorp's journey back to the farm.

Thorp planned to buy a new uniform and surprise his fiancée, Mary Ellen Harris, by showing up unannounced in Wapella. When he couldn't find the uniform, he boarded the Green Diamond for the one-way train trip to central Illinois.

As Thorp left his seat for the platform, he saw that the surprise was on him. Watching patiently as the passengers left the train, Mary Ellen searched for her beloved pilot. Knowing that it would take several days for him to arrive once he made it back to the United States, she went to the station and met every train, hoping that he would be on board.

"As she saw me, I gave a weak salute with a drum in my throat. Many a time it seemed a dream unlikely to come through or true. Home is my home," Thorp wrote in his wartime journal.

During his extended leave, Thorp and Mary Ellen married. She accompanied him to the Army Air Force Redistribution Center in Florida. It was time to decide on whether he would remain in the military. The growing demands of Thorp Seed Company, operated by Thorp's father and brother, were behind Thorp's decision to leave the military. He continued his service in the Air Force Reserves and retired as a captain. Back in DeWitt County, Thorp never gave up his love of flying. Thorp Seed Company maintained the county's largest landing strip, with planes that played a key role in the

In 2011, at age ninety, Ernest had the opportunity to sit at the yoke of a B-17 bomber once again.

agricultural business. Three of Thorp's five children learned to fly, and the family were active in the Flying Farmers for many years.

Thorp was proud of his military service and seven decades as an aviator, with more than seven thousand hours of flight time. He spoke to school and veterans' groups about his experiences. In his late eighties, Thorp noted that he was still legally qualified to fly his Cessna 150 and Cessna 182 for another year. "Who knows—at my age, who knows? So, I'm doing what I've always dreamed I wanted to do."

BOB RYBOLT

SERVICE PILOT

Bob Rybolt's friends would tell you that there were few things he shied away from while seated in the cockpit of his 1949 Piper Clipper.

There's the story of Rybolt flying sideways between two grain storage bins as his cousin, a witness to the heart-stopping stunt, watched from the ground on a patch of farmland in southern DeWitt County. The pilot's son Roger Rybolt believes that a foolhardy bet was behind the maneuver.

"I know my dad was a daredevil. Another pilot told me once that 'Your dad would do things with an airplane that I wouldn't even entertain a thought of doing.'"

As a teenager, Rybolt "wanted to learn to fly and he found a way to do it," said his eldest son, Robert Buchanan. Rybolt's appetite for aviation developed quickly. His acquaintances included stunt pilot Red Irwin, a flyer from nearby Hallsville recognized for his "Flying Circus," a one-man enterprise that introduced locals to the joy of riding in an airplane for the reasonable sum of two dollars.

Another account has Rybolt performing spins and dives over the clock tower of the courthouse in downtown Clinton, causing a panic in the streets below. "Dad said, 'I could see clearly as I was spinning around and coming down, the people looking up and running into stores.' I'm sure he enjoyed it a lot," the pilot's son recalled.

Spectators had good reason to be shocked. Buchanan said, "He was flying against a stiff wind and throttled backward. This made it look as if he was flying backward across the landscape."

For a dozen years, the young Rybolt made a living working on grain and livestock farms. In his early thirties, he landed his first aviation job working as a flight instructor with Clairborne Flight Academy in Wickenburg, Arizona. For a year, Rybolt trained cadets in single-engine aircraft.

Bob Rybolt.

Among items in a storage shed on the Rybolt farm, Buchanan spotted a pair of goggles left over from his father's time in Arizona. "I asked him why the word *look* was written on them. He said that was to remind the students to keep their eyes on him. The training in the open-cockpit planes was all hand instruction, so if they didn't watch the instructor, they were in trouble," said Buchanan.

In 1944, Rybolt joined the Army Air Corps, where his work as a service pilot expanded his experience to the C-47, P-38, B-25 and A-20. Criss-crossing the country, Rybolt relished the chance to fly anything and everything as he ferried planes to training centers, depots for modification and coastal ports for overseas delivery.

When his travels routed him close to home, family members knew when he was nearby. "He must have been traveling from St. Louis to Chicago when he flew over Kenney in a P-38. He called Grandma Rybolt before he took off and said he'd be flying over so she would be watching. She called a couple neighbors, so there were witnesses" who shared the excitement of the farm boy's flyover, at probably four hundred miles per hour, according to Roger Rybolt.

Buchanan was visiting his grandmother that day when "he instantaneously appeared, just above the trees. It didn't last long, but I will never forget it."

Farming endured as the Rybolt family's livelihood after the war, but the fondness for aviation followed Rybolt home. Little was said about his beloved pastime until the Aeronca Champion touched down on the farm, to the amazement of seven-year-old Roger and his younger sister Dona. "I wasn't even cognizant of him being a real flyer when I was young. Then he came home with that little two-seater he'd borrowed from somebody and took us for a ride. Periodically, he would take us up in the evening, when it was calm, late in the day."

In a display of his lingering daredevil spirit, Rybolt introduced his two youngsters to just what a thrill a plane ride could be. "He was just flying along, south of Kenney along that blacktop road, and he asked, 'Is that seatbelt tight?' I told him it was, and he grabbed the tail end and pulled it up. Next thing I know the engines are revving up and we go down and up and upside down and all the way around in a complete loop," said Rybolt.

The after-supper rides above the neighboring farms were a childhood delight for the Rybolt siblings. A short while later, Rybolt bought a Piper Clipper that needed a few repairs and a new paint job. Soybean fields served as a runway as Piper's wheels straddled rows of young crops for a landing. Ruth Rybolt appreciated the ability to fly to Missouri for family visits. Kids from nearby farms were grateful for the occasional ride and the bird's-eye view it gave them of the otherwise mundane landscape.

Reacquainted with his passion for flying, Rybolt looked beyond the acres of corn and soybeans for employment as a pilot. He practiced skimming the tops of fields and skipping over power lines to prepare for a short-term job in the South as a crop duster.

A slightly longer assignment in the frozen region of Michigan's Upper Peninsula caused the Rybolts to pack up the family for a flying gig with an air service that carried people and supplies to Mackinac Island. A newspaper story in the mid-1950s recorded the transport of ninety-nine construction workers in ninety-nine minutes to Mackinaw City. A photograph depicts Rybolt as one of four ski plane pilots to land on ice-covered Lake Huron off Mission Point.

Rybolt kept his beloved Clipper for several more years, flying for the fun of it. Always at ease, whether upside down or level with the ground, Rybolt never lost the sense of joy that blossomed each time he left the ground.

THE CRASH OF A B-17

The sputter of the twin-engine plane stirred farmer David McClimans from his sleep. From his window, he watched as the aircraft struggled through the heavy rain before disappearing into the woods near his farm a few miles southwest of Clinton. The horrific crash that ended with the plane's nose buried into a gravel road also woke McClimans's neighbors. It was just after 11:00 p.m. on February 6, 1943, when the B-25 sheared treetops and barely missed a nearby farmhouse during an attempted forced landing, according to army investigators.

The muddy road leading to the wreckage proved too difficult for the four ambulances that arrived on the scene. Horse-drawn wagons were summoned to the site by sheriff's deputies and army officers, who loaded victims onto carts for a portion of the ride from the crash site. Five victims were identified: Army Air Corps Second Lieutenant Leland Reynolds, forty, of Rochester, Indiana, the pilot; Staff Sergeant Lloyd B. Oliver, twenty-five, Salisbury, Massachusetts, crew chief; Aviation Cadet Walter L Halerz, twenty-two, Chicago; Aviation Cadet John Weldon Gayle, twenty, Bellaire, Texas; and Aviation Cadet Carroll W. Hooe, twenty-seven, Louisville, Kentucky.

Army Air Corps officials said that the transport plane was one of three on a routine training mission from Hondo Air Base at Hondo, Texas, when it became separated from the others and was lost in the stormy weather. The other planes landed safely at Scott Field about 130 miles south of the central Illinois crash site.

Relatives of four of the victims and one hundred others gathered in a cold drizzle on a Sunday in mid-June 1950 to dedicate a granite monument in

Second Lieutenant Leland Reynolds of Indiana was the pilot of the B-25 that crashed in a wooded area, killing all on board.

honor of the army airmen. Before the stone marker was erected on a farm owned by John and Lois Gibson, a handmade sign created by Lois Gibson denoting the loss hung on a picket fence near the crash site. Families of the deceased flyers participated in the creation of the marker featuring a B-25.

Among those who attended the service was the pilot's eighty-five-year-old father, Shuyler Reynolds, and his brother Ralph Reynolds. Reynolds was remembered for his service with the U.S. Marine Corps in World War I. He took up flying after his discharge and worked for seventeen years as a commercial pilot for John Deere. He later enlisted in the Royal Canadian Air Force serving as a transport pilot but transferred to the Army Air Corps when the United States entered World War II. He was retained as an instructor at Hondo, Texas, after taking a training course at the facility.

GENE ARMSTRONG

AEROSPACE ENGINEER, NASA CONSULTANT

When NASA took its first steps toward man's journey into space, Gene Armstrong was there, serving as an advisor to the fledgling endeavor. Armstrong's experience dates to his time as a navigator of B-17s during World War II.

Armstrong was shot down twice during his two years with the Army Air Corps. Injuries suffered during the second incident sent him back to Illinois, where he finished his degree in aeronautical engineering.

A career working on guided missile programs took Armstrong to locations around the country far from his family in Clinton, Illinois. General Dynamics recruited Armstrong in 1954 as part of its Convair Division working on the Atlas ballistic missile program. By 1958, he was chief engineer, responsible for training five hundred young engineers—all of them under age thirty-two—who would design and fly the Atlas launch vehicle. During the planning stages of the newly formed National Aeronautics and Space administration, Armstrong was one of the leading experts named to the Research Advisory Committee on Control, Guidance and Navigation, an assignment that would last three years.

"During this period, the United States was hastening to win the Space Race, with most of the leading technical personnel of the country on panels and committees to advise the government," Armstrong wrote in a summary of his career.

The advisory panel's "function primarily laid the groundwork for the Apollo lunar landings ten years later," according to Armstrong. As chief of the Dynamics Division, Armstrong spent almost half of his time on special assignments, including seven months at Cape Canaveral in Florida overseeing all electronic systems for the first three Atlas launches.

As the country moved closer to putting a man in space, Armstrong and his colleagues took on the burden of creating a safe and reliable system to accomplish goals that seemed as unreachable as the stars a decade earlier. "It was apparent the United States was entering into manned space, with only partially proven system of unknown reliability," Armstrong noted in his work summary. He was assigned to a committee set up by President John F. Kennedy to "ensure the maximum success of the Mercury Program, while at the same time responsible for the Atlas Booster."

In June 1963, Armstrong took over as chief engineer for the Centaur, a space vehicle developed by NASA. The project came with uncertainties, as questions were raised about the vehicle's high-performance hydrogen-oxygen engine and guidance system. Solving guidance problems and other tough issues was Armstrong's strong suit.

"The first completely successful flight was accomplished within six months with another following within the next six months," Armstrong recalled.

Circa 1958, Gene Armstrong (*third row*) keeps his fingers crossed during an early launch of the Atlas rocket at Cape Canaveral.

Centaur's performance laid the foundation for future lunar landings and met NASA's goal of putting two thousand pounds of spacecraft on the moon ahead of manned landings. Armstrong's career with General Dynamics ended in 1965 after he moved to TRW Inc. as manager of Program Development for the Space Vehicles Division in Redondo Beach, California. Armstrong found himself once again asked to resolve major technical headaches—this time with the Minuteman III missile program.

"I headed the 'get well' program," for the missile system," Armstrong noted. Within six months, the system's reliability and performance exceeded all contract requirements, and five hundred missiles were ready for deployment as scheduled.

Armstrong retired in 1986 and died in November 2006 at age eighty-four. A 1965 award for distinguished service in engineering from the University of Illinois recognized the nearly forty years Armstrong devoted to aeronautics: "Mr. Armstrong has had a major role in the missile and space efforts in this country, and his contributions to our nation's first intercontinental ballistic missile system are outstanding."

FLYING FARMERS

Young men who left their family farms to become pilots during World War II returned with new skills that changed the face of agriculture as airplanes joined tractors and combines as essential farm equipment.

Whether taking to the skies to pick up parts or check on livestock and irrigation systems, farmers and ranchers relied on planes to make their operations more efficient. What started out as an idea for a magazine story in 1944 for H.A. Graham, director of Agriculture Extension at Oklahoma Agriculture and Mechanical College, and Ferdie Deering, farm editor of the *Farmer-Stockton* magazine, became the catalyst for a national organization for farmer-flyers.

The National Flying Farmers Association linked thousands of farmers from across the United States through their shared practice of using planes in everyday farm chores. Annual conventions kept members updated on new aircraft specifically designed for their needs. The Silvaire—an all-metal, four-place model—was designed in 1947 by Luscombe with the farmer in mind. In 1948, Cessna promoted its Cessna 190 and 195 to farmers as the industry's "newest tool."

The Thorp family's five-stall hangar built with surplus steel from World War II.

Ernest Thorp of Wapella was one of many farmers who came home from war duty with flying experience. He joined the DeWitt–Piatt County Flying Farmers in 1945 and convinced his father that the family's seed company east of Wapella needed an airplane. The Thorps' planes were kept in the five-stall hangar built just north of the seed facility with surplus steel from the war. His first plane was an Ercoup, followed by a Cessna 140 he picked up in Wichita, Kansas.

Nelson Thorp, the oldest of Ernest and Mary Ellen Thorp's five children, was two weeks old when he took his first flight perched on his mother's lap. "Dad would go up a lot and I would go with him. He always said I was a good instrument pilot because I couldn't see over the instrument panel," Nelson Thorp said of his early days as a passenger.

For the Thorp's offspring, flying was part of life on the farm. "We never knew a day without an airplane," said Thorp's youngest daughter, Zelda.

As a teen, Nelson Thorp chose aviation over motorcycles. When Nelson asked his father to help with the cost of a motorcycle, his father told him, "I'll pay for your pilot's license or I'll buy you a motorcycle—not both." Nelson considers the decision to pursue a pilot's license "the best decision I ever made."

When three of Thorp's cousins also expressed interest in learning to fly, his father hired a flight instructor from Champaign who made weekly trips

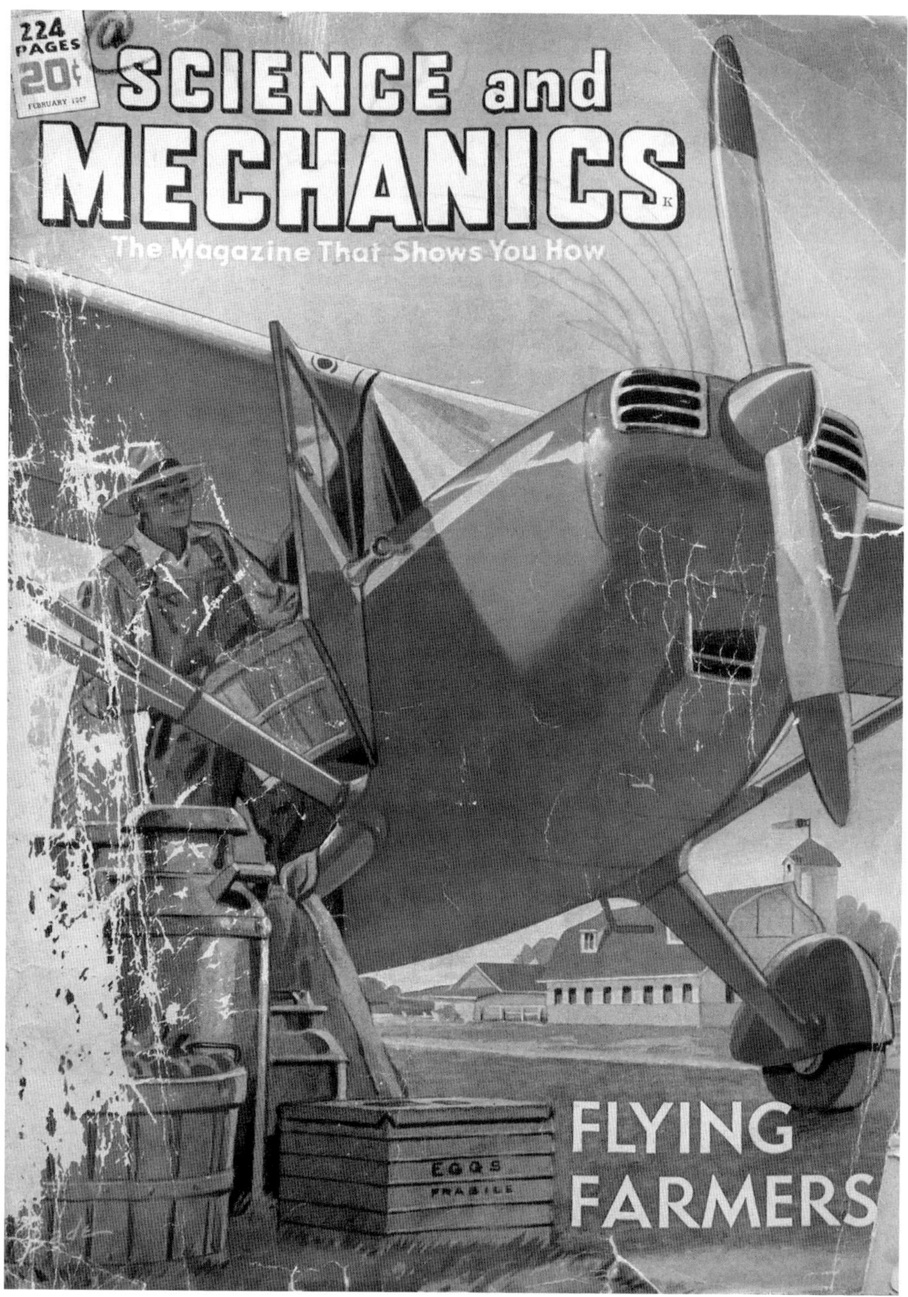

Above: February 1947 cover of *Science and Mechanics* magazine.

Opposite: In 1987, Mary-Ellen Thorp was honored with the title of "Illinois Flying Farmers Queen."

to the family farm. Mary Ellen Thorp served the instructor supper before his return home.

Nelson, Zelda and their younger brother Lewis earned pilot licenses. At sixteen, Nelson completed his first solo flight, and a year later, he became the youngest pilot to fly to the National Flying Farmers annual convention in Denver. Zelda and Lewis rode in the back seat.

The Thorps used their planes like other farmers used their pickups. A machinery part located in another town was picked up in a plane, and fields were surveyed from the air. De-tasseling crews often were treated to a plane ride at the end of their summer employment at the seed business. Airplanes grew in popularity as a tool for farmers across the country.

In 1961, the Flying Farmers organization became the International Flying Farmers and carried a roster of eleven thousand members by the mid-'70s. Mail and groceries were delivered by air, along with livestock feed. Ranchers located missing cattle; perspective land buyers and bankers surveyed farms from airplanes.

For decades, the involvement of families with a love of flying helped IFF maintain its membership rolls. Farmers who made their living on the land and held an almost equal passion for aviation were active members of the IFF, sometimes spanning generations.

The Thorp family, which included daughters Carol and Marjorie, traveled together to conventions. In 1974, Ernest served as IFF president, and Zelda led the group's teen organization. Following in her father's footsteps, Zelda became IFF president in 2017. Flying was also part of her family; her son Douglas is a pilot and works for the Federal Aviation Administration.

As the farm economy struggled, IFF membership dropped. Today, the group has 455 members from 275 families. The expense of owning and operating aircraft has contributed to the lower numbers.

The enthusiasm of current members remains strong for the organization and the role aviation has played in agriculture. "This organization had a rural farm feel from the beginning. It's like the farm community—you have that bond," said Zelda. Her brother Lewis echoed those sentiments: "May the joy of family, farming and flying be forever cherished."

WARNER GASH

U.S. ARMY AERIAL GUNNER

Warner Gash.

A box of faded photographs found under the bed opened a small window into Warner J. Gash's World War II service as a gunner on B-29 aircraft.

At thirty-two, Gash was among the older volunteers to join the Army Air Force in July 1945. As a gunner and armorer, he arrived on Tinian Island with the 483rd Bomb Squadron, part of the 313th Bombardment Wing, with the 20th Air Force.

Firing a gun came naturally to Gash. As a boy growing up on the south side of Clinton, he would take a shotgun and a single slug and go out looking for a rabbit or other game for the family's evening meal. The skill was recognized when he arrived at basic training at Laredo Army Air Field in Texas, recalled Gash's daughter Sharon Redington. "He went to gunnery school in Texas because he was such a sharpshooter at moving targets," said Redington.

Redington first learned of her father's military service when she was in middle school and found a photo of a man in a military uniform in her mother's room. Later, a metal box of photos under her parents' bed shed more light on his time in Japan—images of mass graves of victims of the atomic bomb showed the horrors of war he had witnessed.

The 509th Composite Group was part of the 313th Bombardment Group and formed as a special unit to launch an atomic bomb on the Japanese city of Hiroshima on August 6, 1945, and Nagasaki three days later. The 20th Air Force took its orders directly from the Pentagon on matters linked to the presidential-level team coordinating the Japanese attack. Located 1,500 miles south of Tokyo, Tinian Island's proximity to Japan made it a desirable launching site for bombing attacks.

In recognition for his service, Gash and other World War II honorably discharged soldiers were awarded a "Ruptured Duck" lapel pin. Named for a B-52 that bombed Tokyo in 1942, the lapel button was awarded for service between 1925 and 1948. An embroidered patch sewn onto discharged soldier's uniforms confirmed their military status.

After his departure from the Army Air Force, Gash came home to Clinton, where he worked for the city water department as a stationary engineer.

LEE BAKER

FLYING FARMER

Lee Baker's occupation was farming, but his passion was his service as "ambassador of Illinois aviation."

Baker grew up near Weldon, where his love of flying was kindled by the kites he launched over the family farm. In a handwritten account of his early connection to aviation, Baker recalled his childhood on the farm "watching birds fly and glide and too heavy chickens trying to make it over the chicken yard fence, seeds from maple trees windmilling down to the ground, my thoughts always return to why not someday I could fly."

At age seven, Baker was driving a team of horses behind a three-section harrow when he first heard and then saw an airplane, an unlikely sight over the prairie. The silver and white aircraft turned out to be an airmail plane piloted by Charles Lindbergh, en route from St. Louis to Chicago. "That was a day for me to remember," Baker wrote in his memoir.

After high school, he went to Chanute Air Force base in Rantoul with his heart set on becoming a pilot. Those plans were derailed after his parents refused to sign the required paperwork. Baker's father wanted to retire and pass the farm on to his son.

In 1941, Baker was drafted into the U.S. Army. He served in the 3rd Armored Division of General George Patton's 3rd Army. Baker's wife, Charlene, accompanied him, working as a secretary at military headquarters wherever Baker was serving. He served four years before returning to Illinois and a job at a manufacturing plant in Decatur that turned out parts for the atomic bomb.

Baker and Apollo astronaut Jim Lovell.

Determined to become a pilot, Baker tapped his GI benefits to pay for flying lessons and earned his pilot's certification in 1947. He returned to the family farm and joined the Flying Farmers, a group of aviators who used airplanes in their farming operations. The Bakers flew around the country for Flying Farmers conventions and hosted "fly-ins" at their farm. Baker's daughter, Suzan Schlessinger, and her brother Jim made some of the trips with their parents in the 1947 Stinson 108-2.

"I would get in the back seat and fall asleep. Dad would say, 'You're missing the view,'" she recalled.

The business card Baker carried lists his special interests as "ambassador of Illinois aviation." Special interests listed on the card included space education and kite or rocket composites and demonstrations. He also was known for airplanes he fashioned from pop cans. The metal planes were flown by kites and Baker-made rockets for demonstrations. As a member of the C.H. Moore Homestead and DeWitt County Museum, Baker helped local kids build and fly kites made from garbage bags, duct tape and wooden dowels.

Apollo 13 astronaut Jim Lovell signed Baker's fifty-four-inch Saturn V5 rocket model at a Wings Program held at College Colorado Airport. During one conversation with the astronaut, Baker asked for his opinion on when the United States would return to the moon.

"About the same time it took us to get there—10 years—but we will be there again," Lovell told Baker, according to Baker's memoir.

After Charlene's death, Baker married Harriett Raker, and the two enjoyed taking shorter flights close to home. For their tenth wedding anniversary, the Bakers chartered a DC-3 from the Prairie Aviation Museum for a flight over the family farm, with fourteen family members on board.

In 1995, Baker was inducted into the Illinois Aviation Hall of Fame for his work as an aviation ambassador. He expressed gratitude in his later years for his work as a farmer and the good times he shared with family and friends, "and all will remember I walked among them, always looking up."

ANN HERRICK

PILOT

Amelia Earhart, the first woman to fly solo across the Atlantic, inspired women across the country to join her in the cockpit as the boundaries of aviation extended beyond an all-male endeavor to a growing roster of female pilots.

Recognized in 1948 as one of five University of Illinois "Flying Co-eds," Ann Herrick was among the first DeWitt County women to complete flight training. The students were the largest group of women to obtain private pilot licenses at the university.

Herrick's training at the school's aeronautical program followed her return to the university after four years with the Women's Army Corps. The daughter of Dorothy and Wirt Herrick, a Clinton lawyer, Herrick also attended the Art Institute in Chicago and went on to teach art in all of Clinton's schools.

The new pilot was one of seventy licensed aviators in the county, according to a 1948 report of registered airmen. Herrick worked as a secretary at the airfield south of Clinton. Aviation lured forty-three others to pursue pilot licenses at the local airport. Five aircraft were used for training the men enrolled in classes. Herrick enjoyed taking off from the local airport with friends on board.

The U.S. State Department put Herrick's skills as an aviator and artist to good use during her tenure as a cartographer with embassies in Athens, Greece; Berlin, Germany; and the Belgian Congo in Africa. She spent two years creating a mural at the U.S. embassy in Leopoldville in Africa.

The largest group of coeds to complete a private pilot license course: Jane Pheiffer, Washington, Illinois; Colleen O'Riley, Danville, Illinois; Leona Speer, Normal, Illinois; Elizabeth Theilemann, Meadville, Pennsylvania; and Anne Herrick, Clinton, Illinois, January 31, 1948. *Courtesy of University of Illinois Archives.*

Known for her independent and determined spirit, Herrick followed politics and participated in rallies for women's rights. When supporters of the Equal Rights Amendment marched near her office in New York City, Herrick changed into her sneakers and joined the assembly. She returned to Clinton after retirement from her work as a graphic artist.

LESTER SPRAGUE

PILOT

Pilots never forget the first time they lifted off the ground, the excitement and exhilaration of being in the air. For the children of pilots, the joy of sitting behind a parent aviator is equally unforgettable.

Lester Sprague was bitten hard by the aviation bug, and with encouragement from his friend Ernest Thorp and many hours of practice, he earned a pilot's license. "Dad was crazy about flying and was taking lessons while we lived at the Valley Mill Farm. We spent many weekend afternoons at Thorp's seed farm, where there was an airplane hangar and a grass runway. Dad started with a flying club, called the Flying Farmers," recalled Sprague's daughter Kate Sprague Gledhill.

"The more Dad flew, the more he was hooked on flying. Dad was finally able to buy a partial ownership in a plane. He would take us flying over the farms and landscape we knew so well from the earthbound perspective, but they became absolutely beautiful from the air, like a multi-colored quilt. My dad loved it, as we all did," said Gledhill.

When Sprague was able to buy his own plane, it was a two-seater Piper Cub. He later traded the plane for a four-seater Cessna made of wood and canvas—"not very confidence-inspiring, but it was a Cessna and that was what he wanted," said Sprague's daughter.

Construction of a landing strip required some creative engineering. And landing the plane after dark involved assistance from his wife. Gledhill explained, "Once he had the Cessna, Dad built a little bridge across the creek to get the plane across to the runway he was building. He built an airstrip running perpendicular to the bridge just down the road from our driveway and parallel to the creek that ran through our place. Of course, the runway was a bit less than a quarter mile long, which did not leave any room for mistakes. When he was landing at night, he would 'buzz' Mom at the house, and she would park, with her car's headlights shining at the end of the runway so he could see to land."

In the early 1960s, Sprague began flying a club of parachutists for jumps over the landscape near his home. "Dad had to remove the passenger side door so they could stand on the wheel mount and jump from there. As our farm was quite close to town—straight east on Washington Street—lots of folks used to come from town to watch the jumpers do their thing. Sometimes the visitors would bring a picnic lunch and sit on the lawn. While the jumpers were repacking their parachutes, Dad would take anyone who was interested in a ride. He never charged them and got a big kick out of taking folks up who had never been in a plane," said Gledhill.

A teenage Gledhill considered joining the parachutists for a jump. "I asked Dad if I could do it, and he looked at me like I had lost my mind. He finally said, 'You come up with us while they are jumping and watch them—then tell me if you are foolish enough to jump out of a perfectly good airplane.' Dad would never even wear a parachute, as he was supposed to with the door off for skydiving. I did go up for one trip when they were doing jumps, and Dad was right. I was not foolish enough to jump out of a perfectly good airplane," Gledhill said.

A much newer Cessna parked behind the Sprague's machine shed also served as transportation for relatives as the pilot "took any excuse to fly," according to his daughter. Family trips to Florida and a college visit to Colorado for Gledhill were a few of the flights Sprague piloted.

Two trips to a school campus in Boulder proved challenging for the pilot and his passengers. During Easter break of Gledhill's senior year, the ice, snow and sleet that blanketed Illinois made landing the plane at home a dangerous proposition.

"There were pretty bad crosswinds as we 'buzzed' Mom, and she sat on the road at the end of the landing strip with her car headlights on. There also was the issue of the fence at one end of the short runway and the overhead electric wires at the other end. The stiff crosswind made it necessary for Dad to line up three times before he caught the wind just right and he could set it down. I never knew him to have to make two passes, let alone three to land, but it was horrible weather. We were all scared, but Mom was frightened so badly she swore we would never ride with him again, but she knew he was a good pilot and never followed through on that threat," said Gledhill.

Sprague's curiosity and his ability to fly sometimes collided, as was the case on May 20, 1964, when he was asked to check out a law enforcement operation that was blocking traffic on a road outside the village of Wapella. The story, said Gledhill, went far beyond the borders of DeWitt County. "Of course, he jumped in the plane and headed up there. The rest was explained in the newspaper. I gather he was lucky not to have been shot down!"

The small-town commotion was detailed in a *New York Times* story about the largest weapons bust in the country at the time, outside of Florida. Sprague witnessed the historic weapons bust unfold from his front-row seat in the air.

DAVID WRIGHT

U.S. AIR FORCE METEOROLOGIST

Greenland, the ice-covered island resting at the top of the globe between the frigid waters of the Atlantic and Arctic Oceans, was the last place David Wright ever imagined he would live when he graduated high school in southern Illinois.

But in the absence of any immediate job prospects or money for college, the military seemed a worthy choice. On August 18, 1952, Wright and his friend Jack Jones were inducted into the U.S. Air Force. Both were seventeen when they left their hometown of Collinsville, Illinois, bound for basic training at Lackland AFB in San Antonio, Texas.

Wright took at least fifty placement tests at Lackland. His test scores gave him a lot of options, but he chose meteorology, a field that required him to travel to Chanute AFB in Rantoul, Illinois, for training. In an autobiography penned for family members, Wright recalled the facilities at the central Illinois military base: "Our barracks always had a layer of soot covering the beds, floors and windows. Several times a day, a belch of soot came out of the cold air return by the entrance to the latrine. It was an 'open bay' barracks with double bunk beds on either side of the aisle. The furnace was a coal furnace that required shoveling into the furnace by hand."

Wright was assigned to the 8th Weather Squadron, part of the 5th Weather Group, a carryover from the Army Air Corps of World War II. In late June 1953, he arrived at Narsarsuaq AFB, fifty miles from the southern tip of Greenland. The airbase built by the United States in 1941 was code named Bluie West One after Bluie, the Allied military code name for Greenland.

Wright wore the patches of the 8th Weather Squadron, a component of the 5th Weather Group of the Air Force Global Weather Center.

Before midair refueling became available, thousands of planes being ferried from factories in North America filled up their tanks on their way to European battlefields.

For Wright, the flight on a C-54 cargo plane from Torbay, Newfoundland, cruised at fifteen thousand feet, with no pressurization. He recalled the painful aftereffects. "My ears were affected and after landing, I couldn't hear anything. Over the next two weeks, my ears opened up with painful rips."

The climate also took some getting used to. In the summer months, daylight covered the base from midnight to 11:30 p.m., compared to thirty brief minutes of daylight in the winter.

Wright's job with the Upper Air Section of weather research known as rawinsonde required the use of a balloon-borne radiosonde to evaluate wind speed and direction, temperature, pressure and relative humidity. Surrounded by mountains and glaciers, the base offered a universe of knowledge and experience to Wright and his crew.

On his flight with a forecaster in a de Havilland Beaver float plane, Wright noted upper winds of 345.6 miles per hour at twenty thousand feet. The pilot gave Wright a chance to briefly pilot the plane after he turned the aircraft's pivoting wheel toward the passenger. At eighty-seven, Wright's voice lifted as he recalled the thrill of his flight on the iconic bush plane. "That was just great. They were so easy to fly, and they had seating for seven people."

Dangerous Moves

During his one-year stay in Greenland, Wright experienced several close calls with death, all of them related to the extreme weather. The average wind speed of 57.5 miles per hour and temperatures that dipped to negative sixty degrees created dangerous working conditions.

The blizzard of January 1954 ushered in winds of 176.2 miles per hour. Unable to leave his workstation for three days and tired of the C rations, Wright decided to attempt to "walk" back to the base across the north–south runway. "That turned out to be a really dumb and almost fatal idea. I went out the south door of the 'R Section,' and the visibility was zero. I couldn't even see our AN/GMD-1A tracking antenna," Wright recalled.

Fifty yards from the building, Wright began to slide on a glaze of ice and was stopped by a mound of snow. A momentary dip in the windspeed allowed him to see the antenna and crawl back to the building. That same day, a Danish soldier was lost after he was swept five thousand feet down the runway and into the fjord as he attempted to cross the runway.

In another incident, Wright was leaving a south-facing inflation shelter with a weather balloon when strong north winds created enough suction to pull the balloon back into the shelter. "I was holding the balloon with my right hand and the instrument with my left. We used a small launching reel to take up the 100 feet of 100-pound test line between the balloon and the instrument. A parachute was also part of the rig. When I finally got out of the shelter, the balloon threw me into a cartwheel, and when I let go of the balloon and instrument, the balloon slowly ascended. I got flipped over and over and over," said Wright, describing the episode that left him motionless for some time on the frozen landscape.

It was not unusual for Wright's fingers to become stuck to the nozzles of gas tanks as he filled the weather balloons in the bone-chilling temperatures.

During off-duty hours, the men played pool or lifted weights in the barrack's day room. Wright spent his time shooting photos of the F-86 and F-86D fighter jets with his Leica IIIF.

Wright considered the food at Narsarsuaq "poor to bad," starting with breakfasts of "cold storage eggs," which were on average more than two years old by the time they were cooked. One morning, Wright watched as a cook simultaneously cracked and dropped four eggs over a grill, "when they just vaporized and the smell was awful." A check of the egg crate showed a date of 1937.

Wright ended his year in Greenland as the top-rated rawinsonde operator in the Air Weather Service worldwide. When he returned to Illinois on leave in July 1954, Wright was met by temperatures in excess of one hundred degrees—quite an adjustment from the arctic climate.

Wright was also greeted by his siblings, including his sister Stephanie Russell of Clinton, Illinois, who was fourteen years younger. She still remembers her exchange with her brother about his departure for an island called Greenland. "I didn't want him to go. I asked him how long he would be gone and he said, 'I'll be gone a long time.' I can remember how sad we all were," said Russell, nicknamed "Cotter Pin" by her brother because she had a tendency to wander away.

Rockets and Balloons

Barksdale AFB in Bossier City, Louisiana, offered the 26th Weather Squadron "bachelor airman's quarters" that were a notable improvement over Greenland's World War II army beds. The Strategic Air Command base with its B-47 bombers was near the atomic arsenal storage.

Wright recounted the precautions used by squadron members: "We used bottled hydrogen to fill our balloons and had to wear ground straps on our legs to prevent static discharges which would ignite the hydrogen." For his final assignment with the military, Wright was transferred to the 6th Weather Squadron at Tinker AFB in Oklahoma. With a mission to serve "tornado alley," the teams of rawinsonde operators were sent to locations across the Midwest to track severe weather during the February–November storm season.

Wright was in the inactive reserves in March 1958, married and strapped for money, when he sent a letter to Pan American Airways about a job. A job posting in the *Navy Times* had been forwarded to Wright by his brother, a navy lieutenant at the time. Wright forgot to include his address, but the airline tracked him down through his air force serial number, which had been included in the letter.

"In the telegram, they simply said to report to Patrick Air Force Base, Florida," said Wright. Next stop for Wright was Antiqua Auxiliary Air Force Base, British West Indies. Living quarters consisted of a four-room Quonset hut with two doors on each end and no air conditioning. The weather station was a World War II squad tent.

The PanAm team recorded surface weather conditions on an hourly basis, twenty-four hours a day. The results were logged and transmitted to Patrick AFB via a submarine cable that ran from Ascension Island in the South Atlantic to Florida. The scope of the observations was broad and included sky cover by cloud types, precipitation, lightning, thunder, temperature and barometric pressure in millibars.

In the fall of 1958, while on medical leave from Pam Am, Wright accepted a position with the U.S. Weather Bureau in Chicago. He would be plotting surface weather maps for the forecasters and typing forecasts on a teletypewriter—new experiences for the meteorologist.

A telegram from Pan Am one year later ended the leave of absence and sent Wright to San Salvador as a rawinsonde operator surface-weather observer. In addition to their normal duties, the crew also launched special rawinsonde balloons for test support for launches at the Kennedy Space Center and Cape Canaveral. The schedule was long and grueling—an average of eighty hours per week.

During his tenure with Pam Am, Wright launched the ARCAR (All Purpose for Collecting Atmospheric Soundings) rockets. The rocket, originally designed to measure high-altitude winds to monitor the spread of radioactive fallout, was launched at least four hundred times between 1959 and 1991.

Wright resigned from Pan Am when he was thirty-one and returned to Illinois to finish his degree in engineering. He was hired by McDonnell Douglas, where work on a full-scale mock-up of the F-4 Phantom was one of those projects.

The arctic weather station was a milestone for the eighteen-year-old, who left Narsarsuaq knowing that his work made a difference around the world. "The information went to other air weather service facilities so they could get a total picture of what was going on. That's what made our job important."

VINCE ASHWORTH

COMMERCIAL PILOT

Robert and Linda Ashworth raised a family of flyers. Ashworth was one of five 1956 graduates of the Farmer City High School class to become a pilot. Ashworth joined the Marine Corps and served with the military police before returning home and working as a chemist for Kraft. He joined his father in farming and used his GI Bill benefits to pay for a pilot's license at Illini Airport.

"He got a strong interest in aviation in the military. He had his own plane, and used it for transportation, recreational flying. He always had a plane," said Vince Ashworth, the pilot's son.

Ashworth and fellow pilot-classmate John West operated the Harris Airstrip east of Farmer City. "Aviation was a hot area at the time, due to the fact we had a bunch of pilots getting out of the military and they had access to excess military planes. Anyone could get into aviation, and they were encouraged to do it," said West, who owned a fertilizer business and worked as a crop duster. Some of the former military planes could be purchased for $1,500.

In the mid-1960s, the Farm City Flying Club owned two airplanes and used two instructors to train a class of thirteen. The club moved to the tiny town of Harris outside of Farmer City, where it grew to fifteen members over two decades.

Ashworth's three children—Sabrina, John and Vince—all took flying lessons. Vince and John became commercial pilots. "I flew whenever possible with my dad," said Vince, who currently works as a pilot for an aircraft management firm in Chicago.

Left: Vince Ashworth and his son Logan.

Below: The Ashworth family: Dave, John, Vince, Linda and Sabrina.

In the early 1980s, Robert Ashworth made friends with pilots at the nation's largest annual gathering of aviation enthusiasts in Oshkosh, Wisconsin. Soon the Ashworth family and other members of the flying club began hosting fly-ins for the aviators on their way to the Wisconsin event. The three-day social gatherings attracted pilots from around the country and residents of Farmer City to the airfield.

Warbirds were among Ashworth's favorite aircraft, according to his son. A 1941 AT-6 used as an air force training plane during World War II was owned by Ashworth, along with a fully restored 1935 Navy N3N open-cockpit biplane.

The Ashworth siblings started working on their pilot licenses as teenagers. Vince flew for a small commuter airline carrying passengers and cargo from Florida to the Caribbean before taking a job as a United Express pilot based in Denver. "I flew to every small airport you could imagine in the Rockies," he said. Starting in 2000, Ashworth flew DC-9s and Boeing 717s for AirTran Airways, based in Atlanta, Georgia.

The morning of the 9/11 attacks changed the world of flying for Ashworth and other aviation workers. When air traffic resumed several days later, "It was eerie. There weren't that many passengers," said Ashworth. Heightened security measures in a world darkened by new threats from the sky did not lessen Ashworth's love of flying or his "lifelong dream to be a pilot."

With more than seventeen thousand hours logged, Ashworth pilots private planes for individuals and families. A typical week may take him from Chicago to Santa Barbara, Miami and the Bahamas.

Before his death at age forty-two, John Ashworth worked as a corporate pilot for State Farm Insurance. Sabrina Ashworth Walsh made her birthday solo flight as a high school sophomore.

John Ashworth's daughter, Mickael Ashworth, is a pilot for a regional airline based in Indianapolis. Her brother, Alexander Ashworth, earned his private pilot and instrument landing certificates. Robert Ashworth piloted his last flight in 2013. His love of aviation, passed on to his children, is his legacy. "He encouraged us to work on our pilot's licenses from a very young age," said Vince.

MAJOR GENERAL FRANK E. WILLIS

U.S. AIR FORCE PILOT

After his graduation from Clinton High School in 1957, Frank E. Willis was appointed to the newly formed Air Force Academy, where he joined the academy's third graduating class. June 7, 1961, held lasting memories for the cadet. Following the graduation ceremony, he married his true love, Clarice.

Willis earned his pilot's wings in 1962 after training at Vance Air Force Base, Oklahoma. He was assigned to the 305th Air Refueling Squadron as a KC-135 copilot at Bunker Hill Air Force Base, Indiana. He served as a KC135 aircraft commander in California before graduating from the Armed Forces Staff College in 1970.

An assignment as C-123 aircraft commander with the 315th Tactical Airlift Wing at Tan Son Nhut and Phan Rang airbases, South Vietnam, followed in 1970.

Frank Willis.

During his service, Willis logged more than fifty-one thousand flying hours in the KC-135, C-123, T-39, C-21, C-141 and C-17. More than one thousand combat flying hours were accumulated in Vietnam.

His military awards and decorations include the Distinguished Service Medal, Legion of Merit with Oak Leaf Cluster, Meritorious Service Medal with Oak Leaf Cluster, Air

Medal with six Oak Leaf Clusters and the Air Force Commendation Medal and Oak Leaf Cluster.

Willis moved up the military ranks after completing his master's degree in management from the University of Nebraska in 1973. He was named brigadier general in 1984 and a major general in 1989. In 1993, Willis retired after thirty-three years of service.

BEV HARTSOCK

RESERVATIONIST

Beverly Hartsock's career options were limited when she graduated in 1957 from Clinton High School, but she knew she wanted to experience the world outside the boundaries of the village of Kenney.

At seventeen, she wasn't interested in getting married, becoming a teacher or joining the ranks of the handful of career fields open to women. "I was trying to decide what to do, and I knew I did not want to live in Kenney. I wanted to see the other parts of the world."

She developed a curiosity about aviation based on her father's friendship and fascination with Hallsville stunt pilot Red Irwin. "I started out thinking I'd like to be a pilot, but I didn't think we could afford the cost. I picked up some magazines and saw an ad for stewardess school. I thought I could probably do that," said Hartsock.

Central Technical Institute in Kansas City, Missouri, offered courses for careers in the aviation industry. After completing the correspondence portion of the classes, Hartsock left home in the dead of winter in 1958 for Missouri. "I learned teletype and scheduling, but the minimum age for the stewardess class was nineteen so I was trained as a reservationist."

With diplomas in hand, students were interviewed by airlines representatives looking for new employees. A Canadian airline was interested in hiring Hartsock as a stewardess and was willing to wait for her nineteenth birthday. In the meantime, she returned to Illinois and went to work for Ozark Airlines, answering the phones in a back room of Peoria airport. "At that time, they didn't have women ticket agents at the counter," said Hartsock.

Beverly Hartsock's high school yearbook photo.

Male ticket agents worked the counter, loaded baggage and directed planes on the runway—all jobs now performed by women. Hartsock and her female co-workers were outfitted with headsets at a long table where they answered phone calls from airline customers. Reservations, including information for connecting flights, were recorded on paper. The seven-dollars-per-hour position paid more than other occupations available to women.

Ozark Airlines got its start in September 1943 with flight services from Springfield, Missouri. Two years later, the airline began flying from Springfield to St. Louis on Beechcraft Model 17 Staggerwings, a biplane with a lower wing that protruded farther forward than the upper wing. Federal licensure from the Civil Aeronautics Board was delayed, forcing the airline to shut down until 1950, when Ozark opened flights on Douglas DC-93s from St. Louis to Chicago, Tulsa and Memphis.

Based in St. Louis, Ozark relied on federal subsidies, a common source of revenue for local services airlines. Federal assistance amounted to $4.5 million of Ozark's $14 million in revenue in 1962. With a fleet of fifty planes, Ozark flew to fifty-seven cities, including twenty-one in the Midwest. In 1959, Ozark had twenty-four Douglas DC-3s and three Fairchild F-27s. The DC-3 was the first commercial aircraft with the fuel capacity to fly nonstop from Chicago to New York.

The three swallows perched on Ozark fins represented the reliable return of the swallows each year on March 19 to Mission San Juan Capistrano in California.

In 1950, a ticket from Champaign to Chicago cost $14.20, and a passenger could fly from Champaign to nearby Decatur for $4.20. The DC-3 could carry about thirty passengers.

Hartsock's plans began to change after she started dating her future husband, Howard Hartsock. She transferred to Decatur Airport in 1959, and the couple made plans to get married. "We had to make some decisions," said Hartsock, about her future with the airline, which did not accept married women as stewardesses.

Beverly Hartsock (*left*), with a second Ozark Airlines reservationist at the Decatur Municipal Airport.

The decision to leave Ozark was made as the Hartsocks prepared for the birth of their first child. She also turned down a renewed offer from the Canadian airline. She stayed in touch with former classmates, including one who worked as a stewardess until age seventy and never married.

The demands on early stewardesses were rigorous, Hartsock noted. In addition to the marriage rules, women could not top 135 pounds on the scale and were expected to maintain well-manicured nails. It would take decades, but the young, slim and single mandates went by the wayside as airlines faced legal challenges in lawsuits alleging discrimination. Later, men were invited to become flight attendants. The work was difficult, said Hartsock, for women "who were treated as glorified waitresses, always being told to keep a smile on your face."

By the time TWA purchased the St. Louis–based airline in 1986, Ozark Airlines had switched to an all-jet fleet, with thirty-six McDonnell Douglas DC-9-30s making up most of its fleet. The last commercial flight of a DC-9 was January 6, 2014, with the Delta Airlines flight from Minneapolis/St. Paul to Atlanta.

LAWRENCE OLSON

U.S. AIR FORCE MECHANIC

Lawrence "Shorty" Olson picked up his mechanical skills working with his dad on a farm outside Weldon on the eastern edge of DeWitt County.

Faced at twenty-one years old with fulfilling his obligation to serve his country, Olson enlisted in the U.S. Air Force in January 1959. His work on tractor engines and other implements back home earned him a spot in technical school at Sheppard Air Base in Wichita Falls after basic training at Lackland AFB, both in Texas.

During his two years as a mechanic with the 503rd Flight Line Maintenance Squadron at Tachikawa Air Base outside Tokyo, Olson worked on long-range military cargo planes, including C-97s, C-118s, C121s and C-124s. The unit of 380, including about 120 mechanics, supported troops stationed in Korea.

Olson was the second member of his family to serve on the air base; his uncle Cecil Brown, also a DeWitt County native, was stationed at Tachikawa in World War II. The thin slate walls edged on the top and bottom with rows of mesh screens provided a unique housing experience for the American soldiers.

An early bout of homesickness became more difficult with news from the Red Cross that Olson's dad, Donald Olson, was battling a blood clot in his lungs. He had a 50/50 chance of survival, the airman was told. "I was a basket case," Olson recalled, as days passed with no word on his dad's condition. His frayed nerves were calmed after he accepted a buddy's offer to take him into town via motorcycle to call home. The health crisis had been resolved.

Shorty Olson and two other mechanics maintain a Douglas C-124 Globemaster during the Vietnam War era.

Letters and packages from home kept Olson and fellow airmen up to date on current events, and the homemade cookies from his mother, Mary Olson, lifted everyone's spirits in the barracks. "My mother averaged five letters a week. I probably hadn't written three or four letters in my life before the service," said Olson. But weekly letters and photos snapped with a camera purchased after his arrival on the base soon became the norm. A chance sighting of Emperor Hirohito in a parade as he rode in an open carriage is part of Olson's photo collection.

Like many other airmen, Olson bought a motorcycle for traveling around the island during free time away from his two-days-on, two-days-off schedule. One of those trips was a two-day trek to the summit of Mount Fuji, Japan's tallest peak at 12,380 feet. A Mount Fiji sunrise filled Olson's field of vision one morning, creating a lasting memory of his ascent. Olson ended his time with the air force at Scott AFB in southern Illinois, where his duties included crew chief of a C-131A medical transport plane that made the trip to Eglin AFB in Florida for an unforgettable event. President Kennedy was among the dignitaries who traveled to Florida in May 1962 for demonstrations of U.S. military airpower.

From a distance of about fifteen feet, Olson saluted the president as he passed by in a convertible. "I remember seeing him as he went by, nodding to us. That stuck in my mind, and I'll remember it to my dying day," said

Olson. Months later, Kennedy would deal with the Cuban Missile Crisis and avert the threat of war.

Olson returned to Illinois and a career in farming, but not without giving brief consideration to an offer from the air force for more training that could lead to flight school. "I loved it. If I hadn't come back to farm, I would have made it a career." Four decades later, Olson returned to Tachikawa, this time as part of an agricultural market study with the DeWitt County Farm Bureau. The airbase, which was closed in 1977, was gone.

Travel, training and an expanded view of the world were all part of Olson's experience as he left Weldon for four years in the air force. The time away from America's shores also deepened his gratitude. "It really makes you appreciate the USA more, without a doubt."

RICHARD SNELSON

PILOT AND AVIATION ENGINEER

As a young boy, Richard Snelson sat on a hillside along the banks of the Missouri River outside Wainwright, where he had a clear view of Jefferson City's Capitol City Airport.

Snelson liked to hang out at the airport and talk with the pilots and mechanics. One of the older pilots asked the fifteen-year-old aviation fan if he would like to join him as a passenger. Snelson learned a few of the basics of flying, enough to whet his appetite for what would be a lifelong affection for aviation.

After a stint in the U.S. Army in Okinawa, Japan, Snelson graduated from the Rolla School of Mines in 1962 with an engineering degree. He moved his family to Sunnyvale, California, for a job at Lockheed Aircraft as an instrumentation engineer on a missile program.

Pilot lessons with Amelia Reed (named for the famous female aviatrix) in California and an instructor in St. Louis, where Snelson worked for McDonnell Aircraft on the Phantom F-4 program, earned him the pilot's license he had yearned for as a young man.

When McDonnell was looking for engineers with experience with cameras, Snelson volunteered for the assignment, not knowing that he would be involved with choosing cameras for the Gemini space project. The equipment needed to withstand the forces of space and be easy for the Gemini crew to use. "We did very well. We had no failures with cameras," Snelson recalled.

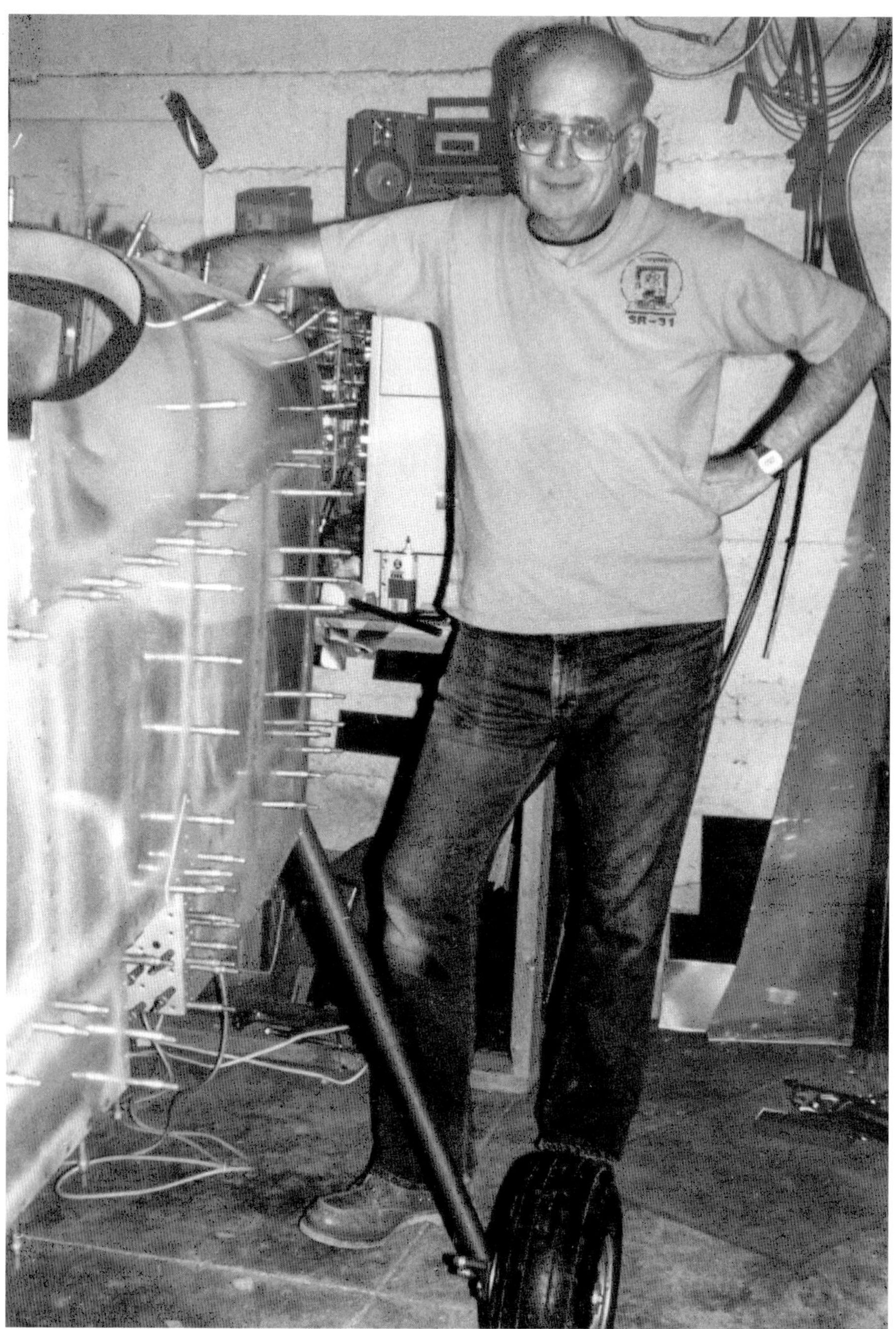

Snelson building his own EAA Thorp T-18 airplane.

Astronauts Gus Grissom, Walter Schirra, Ed White, Frank Borman, James Lovell, Thomas Stafford and John Young were among the crew members Snelson developed a close working relationship with during his time with the program.

The serious and complex work sometimes gave way to lighter moments. Several members of the crew were in the office one day, and Snelson took the opportunity to ask them to sign a blueprint of the capsule's instrument panel. "Thanks for approving the instrument panel," he jokingly informed them, before they chased him down the hall.

The work also took an emotional toll. Snelson left the program after Apollo 1 astronauts Grissom, White and Roger Chaffee died in 1967 when their command module caught fire during a preflight test launch in Florida. Snelson returned home to Missouri and started a stereo and TV business. He continued flying. Cessnas, Tri-Pacers and Cherokee Pipers were all aircraft he enjoyed. Snelson and his wife, RoxAnne, relocated to DeWitt County with their daughter, Courtney, in 1984 for an engineering post at Clinton Power Station, a nuclear power plant outside Clinton.

The dream of building his own aircraft resurfaced with plans to construct the EAA Thorp T-18. The project "was certainly a family a decision as it meant many hours of planning and building and spending money to build 'her' but we were all in for the next 3½ years," said Snelson's wife. The Snelsons met other experimental aircraft builders on annual trips to the Osh Kosh Fly-In. Organized by the Experimental Aircraft Association (EAA), the airshow is the nation's largest gathering for experimental aircraft lovers. One of Snelson's new acquaintances in Wisconsin was Don Taylor, the first pilot to fly a homemade experimental aircraft around the world.

During the later stages of the plane's construction, the Snelsons welcomed an unexpected visitor to their home. World War II pilot and farmer from Wapella, Ernest Thorp, stopped by to see the couple. "He said his curiosity got the best of him when he heard someone was building a Thorp airplane. What a great individual he was, with his encouragement and wisdom, and it was a joy to have him come around to swap information or stories," said RoxAnne.

Others interested in building aircraft came to Snelson's metalworking classes designed to teach the proper method of crafting metal to hold up to the strain and stress of flying.

As the time drew closer for the maiden flight of the EAA Thorp T-18, Snelson prepared for an FAA certification inspection. "It's absolutely critical you document the stages of home-built aircraft," said Snelson.

Snelson began flying again and became active with the Loren Hodge EAA Chapter 274 in Decatur. "We really needed more young people flying," he said. The first Train-a-Pilot program attracted half a dozen "young eagles" who learned to fly Cessnas, courtesy of the chapter.

Flying at 180 miles per hour, Snelson made quick trips to Eastern Illinois University in Mattoon to visit his daughter. He also enjoyed picking up Earnest Thorp and taking him for rides.

In 1995, Snelson was awarded the Experimental Aircraft Award in Osh Kosh and later was honored at the Wright's Brother's Award ceremony in Dayton, Ohio. Snelson and other award recipients were chosen to fly in the U.S. Air and Trade Show in Dayton.

The Snelsons sold their plane in 2001 after logging nine hundred hours as pilot and copilot. "We still look to the skies when other aviators fly by and fondly remember our flying days," said RoxAnne.

DAVID HENARD

U.S. ARMY HELICOPTER PILOT

When David Henard headed off to college, he had three things in mind: aviation, electrical engineering and military service.

As a sophomore at the University of Missouri, Henard learned that joining the Advanced ROTC program and passing the U.S. Army flight physical would enable him to receive forty hours of flight training in a Cessna 150. (Two years of ROTC were required of all students at the university, known today as the Missouri University of Science and Technology.)

The training moved Henard one step closer to his goals. With a father who served in World War II, a grandfather who was in World War I and two uncles in the Korean War, there was no question Henard would follow in their footsteps. "I just grew up feeling like I had an obligation to serve my country," said Henard.

Flight training through the ROTC made a childhood dream come true. "My uncle gave me a set of navy aviator goggles when my future hopes were forming, and that triggered my interest. I joined the Advanced ROTC program because I wanted to fly."

During his junior year, the workload of the engineering program and flight lessons at an airport ten miles from campus was heavy. Lacking a vehicle of his own, Henard caught rides to the airport and often hitchhiked back to campus, where a pile of homework awaited him. "The solo ride came with less than seven hours of flight time," Henard wrote in his 2018 book, *Victory Stolen: The Perspectives of a Helicopter Pilot on the Tet Offensive and Its Aftermath*.

Dave Henard in 2022.

Henard graduated in 1965 and entered the army as a second lieutenant in May 1966. Initially assigned as a signal officer (army aviation began under the signal corps), Henard attended flight school at Fort Wolters, Texas, and Fort Rucker, Alabama.

Henard chose rotary wing training over fixed-wing school because the line for helicopter training had no waiting. Once inside the Bell OH-13, Henard knew that he had made the right choice. "I loved the Huey. It fit me like a glove," he said.

On February 5, 1968, he volunteered for gunship duty with Company B, 25th Aviation Battalion in Cu Chi, Vietnam, a dangerous place to be. Henard was commander of the helicopter providing support for ground troops attempting to retrieve wounded soldiers in the village of Tan Hiep. When the aircraft came under heavy enemy fire, Henard led an assault on a pagoda suspected of containing enemy personnel. After several gun runs resulting in the destruction of the pagoda containing roughly forty enemy soldiers, his door gunner was hit when two rocket mortars struck by a .50-caliber machine gun round exploded, damaging the aircraft. The battle was described in the Distinguished Flying Cross awarded to Henard: "His valorous actions and outstanding leadership contributed immeasurably to the successful completion of the mission and the defeat of the enemy force."

Hundreds of combat missions flown by Henard are detailed in *Victory Stolen*. The author takes exception to the mainstream media's war coverage. He is especially critical of broadcast journalists who opined that the United States was defeated in the Tet Offensive.

Like many soldiers, Henard lost friends and witnessed pain and suffering that would stay with him for many years after his departure from Vietnam. "I don't remember any thrill in my life greater than the one that I experienced on the day that I was leaving Vietnam in one piece," Henard wrote in his book.

Henard headed home in 1969 to attend the University of Illinois for a master's degree in industrial engineering. He worked as assistant director for systems development at the University of Illinois and later served as computer services director at Eastern Illinois University.

Henard retired in 2000 and with his wife, Gail, served with missionary efforts in Scotland, Mexico and central Asia. They moved to Clinton in 2010 to be near their three children and six grandchildren.

HENRY KLEEMANN

NAVAL AVIATOR

Navy Captain Henry M. Kleemann was remembered as a hometown hero after his plane skidded off a rain-slick runway during a December 1985 landing at Miramar Naval Air Station, killing the commanding officer of the Air Test and Evaluation Squadron 4 (XVN-8).

The eldest child of Henry and Catherine Kleemann, he grew up with his five sisters on the family farm in DeWitt County. The Chester White pigs he raised as a 4-H project were shown at the Illinois State Fair in Springfield.

A straight-A student at Clinton High School, he won letters in football and track. He was voted "most likely to succeed" by his classmates. In their eulogies at Kleemann's funeral at St. John's Catholic Church in Clinton, friends and family assured mourners that Kleemann had achieved his dream. Close friend John May said, "I know his life was far from meaningless. He served his country with pride, and he's with God."

Kleemann's uncle, Bishop Edward O'Rourke of the Catholic Peoria Diocese, recalled one of Kleemann's last conversations at home. "One week before his death, he explained to his children his responsibility to protect the earth from war. Henry Martin Kleemann served twenty-one years with great distinction and made a special contribution to world peace," said O'Rourke.

Kleemann made headlines during his military career, beginning with a story in the local newspaper in June 1961 when he was accepted into the U.S. Naval Academy at Annapolis, Maryland. Doris Keane was in her early teens when her brother graduated from the academy. "He was always very bright," said Keane. As for his decision to become a pilot, "his experience

Henry Kleemann.

through the summer training [at the academy] probably had a lot to do with the pick of aviation," she said.

A 1965 entry in the academy yearbook cited "Hammering Hank's" academic abilities and willingness to provide "extra instruction sessions for those of us who were lacking in mental dexterity."

An August 1981 incident involving two Libyan airplanes landed Kleemann on the front page of the *New York Times*. The story detailed his involvement in shooting down two Libyan fighters in the Gulf of Sidra, for which he is credited with the first air-to-air kill in an F-14 Tomcat. At a news conference afterward aboard the USS *Nimitz* with Vice Admiral William H. Rowden, Kleemann used a chart and wooden models of the F-14 to illustrate the defensive maneuvers that took down the planes. "There was no chance that I was not going to pull the trigger. It did go through my mind that it would cause a ruckus," Kleemann told reporters. The decision to respond to the Libyan missile was made quickly by Kleemann, who also had flown in the Vietnam War. "I decided we had been fired upon and they were likely to do it again," said Kleemann.

Captain Kleemann was commanding officer of VXN-8, which was based at the Naval Air Test Center, Point Mugu, California, when his FA-18 fighter slid five thousand feet and flipped, trapping Kleemann inside. The accident occurred during a flight to Miramar for meetings scheduled for later that day. Investigators later concluded that a mechanical failure in the plane's landing gear led to the crash.

During his career, Kleemann was credited with 128 combat missions and was awarded a Bronze Star for valor in Vietnam. Kleemann and his wife, Carol, were parents of four children; Steven, the eldest, is deceased.

The loss of the navy pilot was recognized in tributes by lawmakers in Illinois and Washington, D.C. The designation of a city street as Kleemann Road and an apartment complex as Kleemann Village in Clinton are lasting tributes to the DeWitt County pilot.

Kleemann's family understood his commitment to serve his country and the price he paid in 1985 for his dedication. "He was doing something he loved. That didn't diminish the loss, but it did help us accept it," said Keane.

JAMES KELLY OTTMANN

AIRLINE PILOT

As a young boy, James Kelly Ottmann was mesmerized by the World War II flyboys and their maneuvers over K.I. Sawyer Air Force Base near the center of Michigan's Upper Peninsula. He dreamed of joining them someday.

Following a four-year stint in the air force as an armorer, Ottmann enrolled at the University of Michigan with a goal of becoming a civil engineer. He married his high school sweetheart, Charlotte Ann Lindbom, and before long, the family grew to four after the birth of daughters Jan and Joan.

Ottmann's unremitted love of flying led him to swap a career in engineering—a plan that represented his father's dream for him—for pilot lessons. He went on to work for Zantop Air Transportation, a Michigan-based freight airline for the auto industry. The job required extensive travel for Ottmann and his family.

Joan Rhoades, Ottmann's youngest daughter, recalled moving eight times in the early stages of elementary school. The new pilot was making the most of his dream career. "He was always moving up the ladder. He was a very bright guy," said Rhoades, who lives in Clinton.

The demand for pilots during the Vietnam War created a shortage of commercial airline pilots and an opportunity for aviators like Ottmann. With the age for new pilots raised to thirty-two, Ottmann qualified to begin training to fly a commercial aircraft. He went to work for TWA.

The new job with its potential of more travel initially took a toll on the family. Ottmann's wife stayed behind in Michigan near her family when

Ottmann answers questions from two FAA agents after he was forced to dump jet fuel in a waterway following a bird strike near Boston.

Ottmann relocated to Chicago for his commercial flight training. But after a brief separation and Ottmann's purchase of a home in Hoffman Estates, the family reunited.

The weeklong trips for his domestic flight schedule left the girls without their father for much of their growing years and their mother to carry the full load of parenting, but as Rhoades pointed out, there were perks to having a TWA pilot for a dad. "He was a rock star. He blew the other dads away on the 'Bring a dad to school' days," said Rhoades.

Domestic and international travel was also readily accessible to the Ottmanns because of their connection to the airline. First-class domestic tickets cost five dollars, and international fees were fifteen dollars per person. In addition to stateside travel, the family made a three-week tour of TWA hubs worldwide, including Hong Kong, Athens, Bombay and Tel Aviv. The last leg of the trip from Indianapolis to Chicago was made on a bus after a snowstorm grounded their plane.

After the Ottmann daughters left home for college, the couple moved to Las Vegas, where Ann Ottmann volunteered her training as a nurse to help infants born addicted to drugs.

Ottmann's base with TWA was St. Louis, but he shuttled between the airport and his home for work. At fifty-five, health issues forced Ottmann into retirement from TWA and flying. He was an international captain, flying the L-1011, when he left his post.

In 1995, the Ottmanns moved to Clinton to be close to their daughters and their families. Ann died six months after the move, and Ottmann died in 1995. His affection for aviation never diminished, according to Rhoades. He passed that passion along to Jan, who was ready for a solo flight but did not complete the process because she lacked financial resources for the expensive final portion of licensure.

PHIL RYBOLT

HELICOPTER PILOT

The road from Kenney, Illinois, to Bong Son, Vietnam, was lined with uncertainties for nineteen-year-old Phil Rybolt as he embarked on a plan to serve his country from the air and stay off the ground during his four-year stint with the U.S. Army.

It was 1966 and Rybolt chose flight school over infantry training. His experience with air travel was limited to a childhood flight with an uncle in a two-passenger aircraft near the family farm. Rybolt completed basic training at Fort Polk, Louisiana, and then moved on to Fort Wolters, Texas, for five months of training. He spent four months at the world's largest training installation for helicopters at Fort Rucker, Alabama, learning the skills he needed to operate the military birds.

Many recruits washed out of the program; the delicate touch required to steer and maintain the critical hover position and maintain control of the aircraft proved too difficult. Rybolt mastered the skill in nine hours and graduated from the program on June 6, 1967.

In July 1967, Rybolt landed in Saigon. He was assigned to the 1st Air Calvary Division, 1st Brigade, flying scout missions over areas of active fighting. "They were so short of OH-13 pilots. A lot of them crashed, and some were shot down," Rybolt said of the aircraft. He also flew UH-1, known as "Hueys," the workhorse for pilots navigating the mountainous terrain of Vietnam.

Each day carried a new set of risks that left pilots—most of them nineteen and twenty years old—exposed to severe injury or death. A total of 2,282

Phil Rybolt.

service members were killed while on board the nearly twelve thousand helicopters that crashed or went down by enemy fire during the war, according to the Vietnam Helicopter Pilots Association.

Now retired from more than four decades of flying helicopters, Rybolt recalled the frequent near-misses he saw in Vietnam, "some even before I turned 21." "I turned 21 in Vietnam, and 11 days later, I was wounded," he said, pausing for a moment to let the reality of the statement sink in.

Days started early in the Central Highlands region with "first light missions" from Landing Zone English in Bong Son province. Eight teams consisting of a pilot, gunner and aerial observer took off before dawn for the river areas along Highway One to check for enemy troops on their way back to the mountains after a night of destroying bridges in the area. Infantry troops sleeping on the ground in miserable conditions were delivered supplies and a hot meal by the three-member crews during the "last light" missions. To create landing areas for choppers, chainsaws were sometimes dropped to troops from the air.

Other times, Rybolt flew as a scout pilot with as many as seven on board: a copilot, two gunners, a battalion chief and three other officers from the battalion. He quickly learned that some of his flight school skills could prove more harmful than helpful in Vietnam. For example, he was proud of his

Phil Rybolt in Vietnam.

ability to bring the skids to the ground, soft and deliberate. A maintenance officer set the young pilot straight on the dangers of such landings. "The first time I went in there, and I thought, 'I'm gonna show him my nice, controlled touch,' and he said, 'Don't ever do that. You never know where a mine is or the rotors are gonna blow up and then you're gonna blow up. So don't ever land on the ground if you don't have to.' So that was news," said Rybolt.

The fuse that separated life and death could burn quickly when lit on the battlefield or in the air over Vietnam. The key to staying alive was staying cool and focused during situations that could easily send a person home in a body bag. There were a few incidents that stuck with Rybolt at day's end: a wedding ring spotted from the air on a dead lieutenant's hand or pilots trapped in burning aircraft with no hope of rescue or survival. Rybolt received multiple military honors for his wartime service, all of them in recognition of his willingness to take enemy fire and complete maneuvers to save fellow soldiers in the air and on the ground.

Memorable Missions

On August 17, 1967, an infantry unit needed help after a sniper attack in a rice field near Bong Son. From his position about eight feet above ground, Rybolt spotted a sniper but lost sight of him as he turned the aircraft to give his gunner a better firing position.

"We kept looking, but he shot us before we could see him," Rybolt recalled. Shrapnel from the helicopter's floor exploded and became embedded in

Rybolt's face. The gunner took a round in his foot but did not know he was injured until they made the fifteen-minute flight to a tent hospital.

Two months later, Rybolt's "personal bravery and devotion to duty" were cited in the award of the Distinguished Flying Cross and Purple Heart. Rybolt's helicopter took several hits during an October 1, 1967 reconnaissance mission, also near Bong Son.

On his flight to the division's maintenance and repair base in An Khe, Rybolt encountered tracer rounds fired from a belt-fed machine gun. "I thought, I'm just waiting for him to hit me. I was sure I was hit but I wasn't." Two gunships from An Khe responded to the area of Mang Yang Pass, a narrow steep pass popular with snipers. Rybolt remembered the means he was forced to use that night to provide cover for a downed gunship. A side arm was sometimes the last and best resort.

"I used my pistol. That's all I had. We would run out of ammo, and I would use my pistol. The gunner would fire his out his door. We didn't have anything else to shoot. We had a box of grenades, but that's not a good thing to use when you're trying to get away," he said.

The incident outside An Khe earned Rybolt the Air Medal of Freedom. He was also recognized for his escort of two other damaged aircraft and for marking the enemy emplacements for aerial rocket artillery aircraft.

The Battle of Dak To was a month-long series of conflicts in November 1967 that claimed 376 Americans and wounded another 1,441. On November 13, the 4th Infantry Division came under attack by North Vietnamese forces in a mountainous region covered in brush and vines. Among the mounting casualties was the company commander, who needed immediate evacuation. After a medevac helicopter and supply Huey were shot down in their attempts to land in the single ship-sized space cleared by chainsaws, Rybolt and his copilot considered their options. The maneuver required the pilot to avoid the still-burning Huey and the certainty of mortar rounds.

"I wasn't totally opposed to the idea, but I didn't think we'd live through it," said Rybolt, shaking his head at the lingering disbelief that he survived the ordeal.

With an escort from two gunships to create noise, Rybolt lowered the helicopter straight down and hovered, balancing one skid on the smoldering Huey and the other on a stump. Before the wounded officer could be loaded, Rybolt had to deal with an infantryman, hysterical and determined to leave his unit, who jumped on the helicopter and had to be removed. A second Distinguished Flying Cross was awarded to Rybolt for those lifesaving efforts.

On February 1, 1968, during a rescue mission, Rybolt's scout helicopter took heavy fire during efforts to assist another downed aircraft. Rybolt "made low level passes over the enemy positions while, at the same time, directing the rescue operation," according to an account attached to a Distinguished Flying Cross award.

The DeWitt County native has no regrets about his decision to fly missions that left him injured on several occasions, including the shrapnel injuries that surface to this day in the form of minuscule bits of metal that unexpectedly work their way out of his body. And time has not erased the memories of moving from place to place, in tents with no electricity. "You didn't have to look too far to see someone who was worse off," said Rybolt.

Ann Rybolt, the pilot's wife of fifty-three years, described helicopter pilots as "a breed apart—they are all smart, independent thinkers." The couple dated as teens but went their separate ways—Ann to college and Phil to the military—after high school. An early morning phone call from Rybolt asking for a ride home from the Bloomington airport after his tour in Vietnam reunited the pair.

Ann recounted details of the ride that led to a renewed courtship and marriage: "He was so mad because they wouldn't rent him a car at the airport because he wasn't old enough. He wanted to surprise his folks because he got home a little early."

After his military service, an unexpected request from a member of the Iowa National Guard while Rybolt was a student at Western Illinois University ushered him back into the pilot seat. The unit in nearby Davenport was looking for pilots with experience in flying large, twin-engine helicopters. Rybolt had flown the aircraft, holdovers from World War II, while stationed in Germany.

The National Guard became part of Rybolt's life as he traveled to multiple states and countries for his career with Caterpillar Inc. Search-and-rescue missions in Vermont and New York and flood duty in Illinois were part of the stateside military obligation. By the time he retired from the National Guard in 1997, he had accumulated thirty-one years of military service.

Rybolt extended his time in the air after his 2004 retirement from Caterpillar when he accepted a pilot's position with Air Evac Lifeteam, an air ambulance service. The position required at least one thousand hours in a helicopter. The long-range aircraft routinely picked up patients from small hospitals and accident scenes in Illinois for transfer to Level I facilities.

Crews worked twelve-hour shifts for seven days, followed by seven days off. The medically equipped aircraft has room for the pilot, a flight nurse, a paramedic and a stretcher. The patient bed extends to an area where a copilot would normally be seated, putting the pilot in proximity to what's going on.

Emergency rescue scenes are chaotic and surrounded by potential dangers for first responders. The brief opening in the window of time to shuttle a critically injured victim to lifesaving medical care makes air rescue a preferred option. But weather, unfriendly terrain and power lines can reduce or delay that option.

During a flight on the Bell Jet Ranger, each professional on board had a say in whether the helicopter touched the ground. "There was an air evac rule that anybody—the pilot or the flight nurse or paramedic—anybody who didn't feel comfortable landing at that site, could call it off," Rybolt explained.

A landing was temporarily aborted one night when a nurse yelled "Wire!" after she spotted a power line. The crew is always on the lookout for power lines and relies on firefighters on the ground to shine spotlights on those hazards that may be hidden in the dark. The decisions on weather and aircraft maintenance issues were left to the pilot, while the flight nurse was charged with decision-making related to the patient.

From a weather standpoint, fewer risks exceed ice. "Ice on a helicopter is not good," said Rybolt, admitting, "I've landed them where you could barely see out the windshield." Parking in a remote spot allows the aircraft to safely shed the frozen spears from its blades.

After forty-two years at the helm of helicopters in the United States and overseas, the Rybolts are enjoying retirement in Clinton, a few miles down the road from Kenney.

SKIP ARMSTRONG

HELICOPTER PILOT

Paul "Skip" Armstrong was expecting the letter from the Selective Service—the draft board was summoning young men from all the small towns of DeWitt County, including Armstrong's hometown of Wapella.

At twenty-three, Armstrong was older than many draftees and working for a grain elevator in Pekin loading railcars when his draft number came up in 1966. He and the other future soldiers from the area reported to the R&R Restaurant in Clinton for the trip to the U.S. Army induction center in Chicago.

As part of his basic training at Fort Campbell, Kentucky, Armstrong took a battery of tests to determine his skills for different military specialties. He went on to Fort Knox for advanced training in tanks and armor. While there, he was accepted into Officer Candidate School.

The decision to pursue flight school came after some reflection by Armstrong on the weather in Southeast Asia and the temperature inside an armored vehicle. "I got to thinking, I know I'm going to 'Nam, and it will be really hot inside a tank, so I applied for aviation training."

Like other pilots seeking a safer option than high-risk helicopters, Armstrong's first choice was fixed-wing aircraft. But a shortage of pilots needed for helicopters pushed that choice aside.

After five months training at the army's primary flight training center at Fort Rucker, Alabama, Armstrong graduated in July 1967. His next assignment with a medical support unit in Fort Carson, Colorado, provided Armstrong with about eight months' experience flying in high-density altitudes.

Skip Armstrong (*right*) in Vietnam.

The trip to Vietnam in April 1969 took Armstrong to the 92nd Assault Helicopter Company, based at Dong Ba Thin, near Cameron Bay. The company provided general support to Korean, Vietnamese and U.S. units. When called on, the company's pilots, known as the "Stallions," flew combat missions.

The October 30, 1969 attack on Firebase Kate was a memorable day for Armstrong and the 27 American soldiers and 156 Montagnard militiamen who tried to defend the remote mountaintop outpost. The assault by three North Vietnamese army regiments lasted five days and ended after the American-led defenders exhausted their supply of food and ammunition.

Armstrong and crew were on board a Huey headed to the firebase with personnel and supplies but were forced to turn back after taking enemy fire. "We got 'stitched,'" Armstrong said of the rounds, "but were able to get back to a safe location."

The ground troops managed to escape from the base through enemy lines under the cover of darkness. The evacuation, led by Captain William

Albracht, the youngest Green Beret in Vietnam, saved 150 lives. Armstrong and his crew members also escaped serious injury. "The toe was shot out of my boot," said Armstrong.

When he wasn't flying missions or certifying the skills of new pilots, Armstrong supervised about two dozen enlisted men, many of them still looking forward to their twenty-first birthdays. "The majority of them were still in their boyhood, but within a few short months, they became young men," said Captain Armstrong.

Emotional and physical problems sometimes followed the young soldiers to war. A "Dear John" letter from a girl back home, a throbbing toothache and other unresolved issues were dealt with during regular gatherings hosted by Armstrong. He brought beer and soda for the informal chat sessions.

Noticing the better conduct among the troops, the company commander pressed Armstrong for his secret. "He wanted to know how we had a complete turnaround in our unit."

After his year in Vietnam came to a close, Armstrong returned to Fort Rucker, where he spent the remainder of his four years teaching others how to fly helicopters.

In July 1971, Armstrong took a job with Central Soya in eastern Ohio, a move that led to his enrollment in the National Guard in nearby West Virginia and three more years at the controls of a helicopter. The governor and other state VIPs traveled on flights piloted by Armstrong's unit. Armstrong returned to the family farm in 1976 and lives a few miles from the former Thorp Seed Company, where he spent time as a kid with his friends helping wash planes owned by the Thorps. Few things were more fun than taking a ride over the farm fields.

He stays in contact with friends he made during his time in the army. Social media and biennial reunions bring people together to share memories of camaraderie and survival. "The reunions have been beneficial for some of the guys. Some are apprehensive when they come to their first one, and then after they are there, they become completely different people," said Armstrong.

CHARLES "CHICK" HARRINGTON

HELICOPTER PILOT

That was in 1967. I was in university not doing well," recalled Harrington. "It made me vulnerable to getting drafted." After he passed a battery of aptitude tests, Harrington found himself sitting at a table across from three army majors in uniforms. He remembered the exchange.

"So, Harrington, why should the United States Army spend all this money to teach you to fly a helicopter?"

"Why, I don't care about helicopters. You got any jets?"

"No, the army does not have any jets…but we need helicopter pilots."

After a few months of basic training, Harrington was sent to flight school in Fort Wolters. He remembered that even before they completed ground school, about 20 percent of the candidates dropped out, due in large part to the constant harassment by officers. "They'd ask you dumb questions, and if they didn't like your answer, you were doing push-ups and all that stuff."

Flight training in Hughes 269 helicopters consisted of an intense regimen of ever more complex maneuvers and emergency procedures. Students progressed to instrument and formation flying, cross-country and tactical training and eventually transitioned to the more advanced Bell UH-1 Iroquois "Huey."

After a yearlong training, Harrington was flown in a commercial jet to Japan and then to the Bien Hoa Air Base near Saigon, Vietnam, where he was loaded in the back of a Huey that flew at very low level to avoid artillery passing overhead. "You could see beautiful palm trees just zipping by.…And then we got to Pleiku and we were what's called 'FNGs': F'ing New Guys."

Chick Harrington in 2022.

Harrington mostly flew the Cobra gunship. He remembered that pilots could fly three different types of helicopters: the Hueys to transport troops or pick-up downed pilots, the Cobra gunship or the Hughes scout helicopters, nicknamed "Loach." Pilots had no choice in the matter, except if they wanted to volunteer to fly as scouts, the most dangerous role.

Harrington recalled, "The tour of the scout was six months, five hundred hours or twice shot down. I mean we lost a lot of scouts all the time. They got picked up mostly. Mostly, but not always. Basically, you're a fishing lure. You'd go out there and hover around the trees. When they shot, you'd get out of the way, and the gunships would beat the hell out of the area."

On one occasion, on a scouting mission, Harrington's helicopter was shot down, and his observer was killed. "I didn't know he was gone until I turned around and there he was until I came back and pulled him out. Climbed into the other aircraft and off we went. And it burnt up right there."

Harrington had heard that Air America pilots earned five times as much money as army flyers. While still on his tour in Vietnam, Harrington sent in his résumé on a whim in response to a magazine job ad. "It was in ballpoint pen on notepad paper, and I sent it in."

It wasn't until more than a year later that Harrington was invited to an interview in Washington, D.C., followed by a lengthy written psychological profile test. To his great surprise, Harrington found out that he had passed the test with flying colors.

"We had these different jobs. Regular jobs that they did and one of them was to go around and pay the South Vietnamese military. There was a route to these little out-places, and you land and then you pay....Pop out and go to the next location." Harrington said that while it could get dangerous at times, the work was much safer than his time in the army and paid about eight times as much, entirely tax free. Harrington recalled living in a luxurious villa: "I was in Saigon doing what twenty-four-years-old guys do: chasing girls, drinking and hanging out living like lords."

JAMES T. SCHRUM

PILOT AND AVIATION MECHANIC

I grew up in the hill country of Missouri," recalled pilot and licensed aviation mechanic James T. Schrum of Decatur, Illinois. "We lived out on a farm with my grandparents. It was a good life and I grew up busy, with lots of things to do, plenty of boyhood adventures. I didn't know we were poor until we moved to St. Louis when I was a teenager."

"We lived way out in the country," Schrum continued, "and my mom made a point of taking me and my sisters to the library in town on a regular basis. Whenever we went to town for groceries, we went to the library. She made a reader out of me. Books brought the world to my back door. I taught myself a lot, too, just by reading. If you can read and comprehend, you can do about anything!"

Jim Schrum sewing cotton fabric to cover the tail surfaces of a Boeing Stearman biplane.

"Taking things apart to see how they worked," Schrum said with a smile, "well, that was my idea of fun. Mechanical stuff just interested me." Schrum remembered the gasoline-powered Maytag washing machine with a kick starter from his boyhood days. "It had an itty-bitty little engine. I took it all apart to see if I could put it all back together again. My mom walked in and saw what I was doing." Dolly Schrum was upset when she realized that her twelve-year-old son had taken apart the family's washing machine. "I put it back together quick," Schrum laughed, "and I never took it apart again."

"A Machine that Could Take Me Someplace"

Soon, Schrum's grandfather bought him a five-horsepower Briggs and Stratton engine, which the boy disassembled and reassembled repeatedly, eventually mounting it on the front wheel of his Schwinn bicycle. "It worked, but I could pedal faster. But that didn't matter, really. I had a machine that could take me someplace."

Around Potosi, Missouri, Schrum was the only kid with a motorized bicycle. And along the way, he was teaching himself mechanical theory and engineering. Before long, Schrum's fascination with moving parts combined with a love for flight. A neighbor, an engineer for the Illinois Central Railroad who also happened to be a pilot with his very own airplane, took Schrum up for a ride.

For many flyers, the aviation bug bites early, and it bites hard. For Schrum, that one ride was all it took. Soon he and two other friends were part owners of an L-2 Taylorcraft "Grasshopper," a high-wing, fabric-covered, two-place airplane used by the army for aerial observation during World War II.

In 1941, the U.S. Army Air Force ordered four Taylorcraft observation aircraft. They were evaluated in the summer of 1941 during maneuvers in Louisiana and Texas, where they were employed as light transport and a courier—a sort of aerial errand-runner. General Innis P. Swift, the commander of the 1st Cavalry Division, coined the "grasshopper" nickname after watching a Taylorcraft make a bumpy landing in a pasture.

Throughout World War II, in every combat theater, the army used the Grasshopper to spot enemy formations and direct artillery fire. After the war ended, surplus L-2 Grasshoppers became available on the civilian market, and they changed hands at very affordable prices.

"That Taylorcraft flew slowly and had big windows," Schrum explained. "It was just right for going places and sightseeing. It was easy to maintain, too." Schrum fell deeply in love with aviation, but he chose railroading as a career for practical reasons. "At the time, the railroad was more secure employment than aviation," Schrum said.

After getting laid off from the railroad a few times, Schrum picked up his certification as an aircraft mechanic to keep food on the table and to keep him in the air. "I got started with the mechanical end of flying so I could afford to fly," Schrum said.

Many pilots become aviation mechanics out of necessity. Love of flying leads them to the mechanical side of aviation. Maintaining their own aircraft in accordance with federal aviation regulations is the only way they can afford to fly. This may be a particularly American way. After all, in this country there is a long tradition of "do-it-yourself" repairmen who maintain their own vehicles. They are called "shade-tree mechanics."

A veteran of the Vietnam War, Schrum went to college on the GI Bill. He attended Parks College of Engineering, Aviation and Technology in East St. Louis, Illinois. Parks Air College was established by Oliver Parks in 1927 and was America's first federally certified school of aviation, holding FAA Agency Certification No. 1. With two instruction aircraft based at Lambert Field in St. Louis, Oliver Parks started as the sole flight instructor. In 1928, he acquired one hundred acres in East St. Louis and established an "airport campus" of five buildings and two intersecting sod runways. By 1929, Parks was operating thirty-five Travel Air trainers and had an enrollment of six hundred students.

Parks students manufactured their own series of biplane aircraft and for a short time marketed them as the Parks P-2A. The college didn't stay in the aircraft manufacturing business for long; Parks sold the P2A manufacturing rights to the Ryan Airline Company.

This intensive, rigorous training offered at Parks came about as the result of hard experience. Too many self-taught flyers didn't understand aerodynamics—the physics of flight—and they were killing themselves as they attempted to learn to fly. It was apparent to one and all that aviation was too serious an undertaking to be left to amateurs or the uneducated.

Consequently, in 1929, the Civil Aviation Administration (the predecessor to the Federal Aviation Administration) came into being. The CAA standardized flight training procedures. Performance standards were established; CAA testing evaluated a pilot's aeronautical knowledge as well as practical skill operating an aircraft. At the same time, the CAA developed a training and licensing regimen for airplane mechanics and technicians. In the 1930s, Parks students enrolled as aeronautical engineers were required to design, construct and test fly their own aircraft.

In 1931, Parks offered an executive transport pilot's license. In 1935, the college started Parks College Airline, a student-run airline operating a single route between the college and Chicago, Memphis, Indianapolis and Kansas City. By 1936, the Parks training fleet had reached a total of forty-nine aircraft.

In 1938, the Army Air Corps asked Oliver Parks to establish a Civilian Pilot Training Program, complete with barracks and a fleet of aircraft, to provide basic training to thousands of pilots. The effort was enormously successful; by the end of World War II, more than thirty-seven thousand cadets (more than 10 percent of the Army Air Corps) had received their primary flight instruction through the Parks training program.

At war's end, Oliver Parks realized that future aviation leaders needed a broader, more academic education, and in 1946, he donated the school to St. Louis University. Now known as Parks College of Engineering, Aviation and Technology, the school continues to this day and ranks among our nation's premier education institutions in the field of aviation.

"When I went to Parks," Schrum recalled, "I got a job at an all-night gas station. I went to school during the day and worked at night. During the 'graveyard shift,' from about midnight to early morning, I did my studying. It wasn't easy," Schrum concluded, "but that's how I did it."

Schrum graduated from Parks College at the top of his class and earned FAA certification as both an airframe and power plant mechanic—basically, the equivalent of a master's degree in mechanical engineering. The certification authorized Schrum to service and repair aircraft engines and to perform maintenance and repairs on the airplane itself.

An Expert Mechanic

After a few years of practical experience in the field, Schrum went back to Parks College for further study. He graduated the second time, again at the top of his class, with his inspection authorization—the equivalent of a PhD in mechanical engineering and aeronautics. This level of training authorized Schrum to perform "major repairs and alterations" and to "inspect and approve aircraft for a return to service"—in simple terms, just about any sort of repair or modification, even building an airplane from scratch.

With a pilot's license and the full slate of mechanic's licenses, the hillbilly boy from Missouri advanced himself to the top of the aviation game. Schrum has worked on cargo planes, helicopters and modern jets, but he prefers older airplanes. "I like the sound of 'round' engines (the big radial, piston-driven engines). They just exude power. A radial engine airplane compared to a jet airplane is like comparing a steam locomotive to a diesel locomotive," he said. "The steam engine sounds musical."

As he sat and recalled, Schrum recited the names of the aircraft he had serviced like a grandfather recites the names of his grandchildren. The oldest aircraft engine Schrum has repaired is a 1925 five-cylinder Lambert radial. "There were only two in existence." Schrum said. "The company went out of business in the 1930s, and no parts were available. I had to fabricate everything we needed. And then I had to obtain FAA approval to install them."

"Working on an airplane is not like working on a car," Schrum explained. You don't just take off a broken part and put on a new one. Everything you do must comply with federal regulations. You must account for every repair or alteration in the aircraft's logbooks. Aircraft logbooks provide the history of all the maintenance that has ever been done on an aircraft. A mechanic following me will look over the books, read all of my entries and continue from there."

Over the years, Schrum said, he found as much satisfaction repairing airplanes as he takes in flying them. "It's a pleasure to hear them run. There's a lot of satisfaction in making something work and run that will take you someplace."

JACK HOLLAND

PILOT AND BALLOONIST

Jack Holland's entry into aviation as a teenager started as a secret mission, financed with the two-dollar hourly wage he earned working on a farm.

As the son of a pilot, Holland knew he wanted to fly. Carl Holland took his son on many flights in the plane he purchased for a farming operation he shared with John Becker near Shirley, just across the border of DeWitt County.

It was 1973 and Holland was a seventeen-year-old student at Olympia High School when he received permission from the school to forgo a work study program to attend a second weekly flying lesson in Lincoln. When he was ready for his solo flight, he invited his parents to the airfield. Holland said, "I kept it a secret because I didn't know how it would go over."

His parents approved of the endeavor, which led to a commercial pilot's certification and the ratings for multi-engine, instrument, sea planes, gliders and hot-air balloon and free balloon (gas) certifications that followed. "Aviation has led me to a lot of things," said Holland, who grew up in DeWitt County but lives on a farm just east of McLean.

Like many farmers who develop an equal passion for flying, Holland found a way to incorporate aviation into his life. A call from a friend living in Florida who was involved in the agriculture flying business put Holland on the path to managing an aerial agriculture application business, commonly known as crop dusting.

Holland's air strip became a satellite location for Curless Flying Service Inc., a large spraying operation based in Astoria, Illinois. Holland was not involved in agricultural spraying as a pilot but also frequently used his planes to shuttle pilots and pick up parts for needed aircraft repairs. "My pick-up truck was a Beechcraft Bonanza," Holland said of his flying workhorse.

Jack Holland.

The spraying season is short but intensive. Starting around July 4 and running through September, pilots are in the air about ten hours per day. The time spent in the hangar loading agricultural products adds to the workday. The rigorous schedule is maintained seven days a week, daylight to dark.

Curless's customer base for the satellite location includes about a dozen fertilizer plants in central Illinois. On one of its busiest days, the operation loaded and reloaded six planes that sprayed sixteen thousand acres. Although the goal is to keep pilots within thirty miles of Holland Field, pilots occasionally fly as far as sixty miles from McLean.

Pilots come from outside Illinois to work with the aerial application crew. The business attracts pilots from states like Louisiana, Florida and Arizona, where the busy season is the opposite of central Illinois' farming schedule.

Holland has retired from farming and management of the crop dusting operation, but a lease agreement will allow Curless pilots to continue to use Holland's facilities. Holland still flies for fun, about seventy-five hours each year, in an American Champion Scout housed on the property. Flying, he said, serves as "a stress reliever."

One of the planes previously kept in Holland's hangar was the Vans RV-7 he built from scratch. The two-year project was completed in February 2005.

A flight from central Illinois to DuPage County in a PT-17 Stearman with a special passenger on board holds special memories for Holland. "One of the greatest things was when I took my dad flying," he said. Holland had flown the biplane from Alabama and stopped on route to DuPage County. His father, the inspiration for his love of all things that take flight, enjoyed the ride.

A New Flying Adventure

After years of piloting various types of winged aircraft, a ride in a hot-air balloon turned his attention in a new direction. "After the ride, I said, 'Where do I get one?'"

Holland, who logged five thousand hours during almost fifty years of flying, bought a Cameron V-77 and then later a Cameron O-77 and set his sights on the oldest form of air travel.

In 1999, Holland accepted an invitation from his friend Jim Herschend, of Ozark, Missouri, to serve as copilot of a helium-filled balloon for the RE/MAX Cup National Gas Balloon Race. The two set off in Snowbird at 10:30 p.m. on November 6 from Front Range Airport near Denver. At the time, the race to see how many miles a balloon could travel nonstop featured the first gas balloon in Denver since 1936.

Sixteen competitors joined the race across the landscape, traveling north and east, away from the Colorado mountains. A video captured portions of the three nights the pair spent in the gas-filled balloon. Asked by Herschend for his thoughts on the second day of the journey, Holland said, "Get as far as we can, as fast as we can, avoiding the water." The flight path took the balloon over Lake Superior—a ten-hour trip above frigid waters. The sunrises and sunsets were remarkable. With zero light pollution, the view of the Northern Lights was unsurpassed. "You are up there with the stars," recalled Holland.

Holland and Herschend took turns napping and keeping watch as the trip stretched into its third night. The team evaluated when and where to end the race, based on weather conditions monitored by a meteorologist who worked with a three-member ground crew. "You've got to decide what layer of wind you want to be in and your speed. You really are making decisions on the go," said Holland.

As the balloon drifted into eastern Canada toward Quebec, Holland and the pilot found themselves 11,600 feet in the air, traveling fifty-five miles per hour. The cloud cover did not ease until shortly before Snowbird's final descent. When the pair landed in a wooded area near Dolbeau, Quebec, they had traveled 62.17 hours over 1,671 miles, a finish that put them in third place for the race. About 16 miles from the nearest town, the balloonists walked 6 miles to a road where they met two men who helped them transport the balloon to a nearby town, where the ground crew was waiting. The next morning, the Canadians and the chase crew recovered the balloon from the remote landing site to the nearest road for loading in the recovery vehicle for the drive back to Denver.

Herschend and Holland's balloon landed in a remote forest in Maine.

The top team in the Denver race logged 1,783 miles in sixty-five hours, landing in Maine. The third-place finish qualified Holland and Herschend to compete in the Gordon Bennett Cup the following year in Belgium. The oldest gas balloon race, the Gordon Bennett Cup, was sponsored by James Gordon Bennett Jr., owner of the *New York Herald* newspaper. Fall farming obligations kept Holland from joining Herschend for the overseas race. Holland continued to participate in balloon events, although none took him as far as the trip across the United States and Canada.

BOB BALLENGER

ILLINOIS ARMY NATIONAL GUARD

Bob Ballenger has seen the world through the windows of a helicopter dubbed "Magic" by the crew who accompanied him on missions for the Illinois Army National Guard.

After he spent seven years with the Illinois Army National Guard, a friend suggested he join the guard's air division. Helicopters, specifically the UH-1 nicknamed "Huey," were the aircraft Ballenger was assigned as flight engineer before transferring to the National Guard's first Chinook company based in Peoria.

As flight engineer, Ballenger was responsible for a comprehensive preflight check. He made the final call on whether the aircraft was ready for takeoff. Potential mechanical issues are scored and tallied to determine the level of risk. "Nothing is insignificant," said Ballenger, "even a small scratch on a blade the size of a pinhead. At supersonic speed, that's enough to make the blade come apart and send pieces flying like missiles."

Bob Ballenger army portrait.

Ballenger described the Chinook as "an aerial semi-trailer truck," capable of hauling any piece of equipment or armament used by the military. Each load has specific requirements for stabilizing and securing the equipment before

Bob Ballenger at Hooterville Airport.

the helicopter lifts off the ground. The flight engineer, using an altimeter in the back of the aircraft, guides the pilot on altitude and direction.

Sometimes things go wrong, and the flight engineer must use what is called a "pickle switch" to drop the load before landing. Ballenger was forced to use the maneuver during a mission in Joliet after a pilot refused to slow his approach. "When you're fifty feet off the ground and you're coming in at fifty knots, that's way too fast," Ballenger said of the decision to dump military equipment, valued at $2 million.

There was no second guessing of the decision by IANG officials "because it is the flight engineer's decision and lives were saved," said Ballenger.

Ahead of a flight for the mayor of Chicago and an entourage of thirty dignitaries, a mechanical problem grounded the Chinook. The flight was delayed for two hours until a bolt needed to repair a swash plate was delivered from Peoria. Ballenger has no regrets about ordering the delay or placing the red "X"—a symbol that the Chinook was unsafe to fly—in the logbook.

The 106th Aviation F Company was deployed to the Yucatan Peninsula, Panama and Belize to provide military support. The unit spent six months in Honduras providing transportation service to local troops. The Big Flood of 1993 sent the unit to help residents in southern Illinois. "We were in Galesburg for an air show when we got the call. They said we had to go pick up sandbags. We were the first helicopter down there," said Ballenger.

During the three-month assignment, Ballenger's crew picked up nurses on the western shore of the flooded Mississippi and transported them in the thirty-two-passenger chopper for their work in the water-ravaged towns near Alton. "We worked ten-hour days. We lifted a lot of sandbags, carried cargo to troops, food and water."

A winter training in Norway where the local Home Guard taught Illinois guardsmen how to survive in snow-lined trenches is among Ballenger's most memorable assignments.

Six months after his 1996 retirement as a sergeant first class, the guard unit asked Ballenger to return as part of Operation Desert Storm. With two young children, and lacking the requisite physical and flight certifications, Ballenger declined the request to rejoin the unit.

After twenty years of service, Ballenger recommends Illinois National Guard as an option for young men and women looking for a way to serve their country. "It takes a chunk out of your life, but I'm glad I did it. If they call you up, you go. That's the way it is."

PAUL SPENCER BAILEY

AEROSPACE ENGINEER

Perched on his grandfather's lap, three-year-old Paul Spencer Bailey was mesmerized by the full moon resting above the treetops on the farm just north of Kenney. "I threw a rock and missed that bright full moon. I asked my grandad to tell me about it. He said no one could reach the moon—it was too far away." Tom Spencer laughed when his grandson took aim again, missing a second time. "I thought to myself, someday I'm going to hit the moon with two more rocks, one for me and one for grandad," said Bailey.

It was 1955, fourteen years before Apollo 11 would bring astronauts to walk on the surface of the moon, a feat few people could imagine. The moon and the world beyond the treetops were never far from Bailey's mind. As a child, he knew that his less than perfect vision precluded him from being an astronaut, but there were other avenues that could satisfy a space enthusiast.

"When I was six or seven, I learned there was something called an engineer," said Bailey. The job description fit Bailey perfectly: work to develop the technology to put people into space. Following his graduation from the University of Missouri, Bailey worked for two years at the Naval Weapons Center in China Lake, California. He returned to Clinton and completed a master's degree in aerospace engineering at the University of Illinois.

Opposite: Paul Bailey.

Above: Bailey checking out Elon Musk's Starship SN15 in Boca Chica, Texas, 2021.

Bailey began his career at Johnson Space Center in 1978 as an engineer with McDonnell Douglas where he was assigned to the Skylab space station project and the efforts to create a maneuvering unit for untethered spacewalk. As an orbital mechanics specialist, Bailey helped trained astronauts to fly the Manned Maneuvering Unit, a backpack weighing more than three hundred pounds that allowed astronauts to fly unanchored from a spacecraft. The technology's potential was demonstrated during a February 7, 1984 test flight by *Challenger* astronaut Bruce McCandless.

The jetpack's technology was short-lived. It was used in the SolarMax Satellite retrieval mission on STS 41-C and in the Palapa and Westar rescue mission during STS-51-A, both later in 1984, and then retired.

Work on the space station intersected with Hollywood in 1984 as the production crew and actors filming the television miniseries *Space* visited the NASA control room. Bailey and other NASA staff met Michael York and Bruce Dern, two stars of the drama. Bailey recalled his conversation with

York during an elevator ride in Houston. The actor expressed amazement at how NASA workers "have everything planned to the finest detail," compared to the easygoing flow of a production set. Bailey made the final cut of the series, as his image is in a background shot of the control room.

At forty-five, Bailey returned to the University of Illinois for doctoral studies in physics. With a PhD in hand, he returned in 2005 to Houston. He is currently assigned to the management team developing new spacesuits for astronauts.

After more than four decades in aerospace, the moon remains in Bailey's field of vision, just a stone's throw away. With retirement on the horizon, his curiosity has not lessened. "I've still got that date with the moon to keep."

SARA SMITH ESCH

FLIGHT ATTENDANT

A variety of things nudged Sara Smith Esch to "Fly the friendly skies" with United Airlines. "What was the lure? The need for change, flying sounded fun, travel was involved, meeting people from all over the globe and viewing the world from thirty thousand feet sounded amazing. I was hooked."

A 1972 graduate of Clinton High School, Esch spent seven years as a flight attendant with the airlines, starting in 1979. Training for the airline position was conducted in United's facility in Chicago. Students from all corners of the country were part of her class. "Learning the ins and outs of each aircraft, safety procedures and emergency training were all part of the process," said Esch.

Initially based in Chicago and later in Denver, Colorado, Esch experienced a new lifestyle as she flew domestic flights for work and spent her free time traveling the globe. "Two alarm clocks, different time zones, different cities and states and living out of a suitcase became my new norm," she said.

The passenger manifests sometimes included well-known individuals: John Travolta, Dick Clark and Donnie Osmond had seats on United flights with Esch's crew.

The stories of ordinary people who booked flights are equally memorable. Tapping sounds from a restroom on an all-night flight caught the crew's attention. Esch recalled the story this way: "I opened the door and to our amazement [there] was a small girl, dressed in a ruffled dress with black patent shoes and white lacey socks. She had pulled down the lid on the toilet seat and was standing on the top of it tap dancing while watching herself in the mirror. She was adorable! We all smiled, closed the door and let her tap away."

A couple bound for an anniversary trip to Hawaii left a lasting impression. Ted and Rose were touched with Esch's gift of two wine glasses attached to a bottle of champagne on behalf of United. One week later, Ted and Rose had seats on Esch's flight for their trip home.

Sara Esch working as a flight attendant for United Airlines.

"Rose placed an object in my hand. It was a beautiful conch shell from Hawaii. They had brought it back, hoping I would be on their flight home. It is a gift I have kept all these years along with the fond memory of these two kind people."

After seven years, Esch left her job as a flight attendant to explore other avenues. "I am still in touch with my United friends and the friends I met along the way. The interesting and diverse people I met and the beautiful world I've seen has given me wonderful memories I will keep forever," said the former flight attendant.

KEN SHAFFER

U.S. AIR FORCE AND COMMERCIAL PILOT

Ken Shaffer seemed an unlikely candidate for air force pilot training. A lanky six-foot-two, the business major appeared to be better suited for the corporate world when he graduated in 1981 from Illinois Wesleyan University. An internship with General Electric Company convinced the Waynesville native that the air force offered more fulfilling options. "The air force needed navigators. I thought at the time, it's just for four years," said Shaffer, now retired after more than two decades in the military and twenty-two years as a pilot with United Parcel Service.

The handful of years he planned to serve help assuage the concerns of family members. "For the most part, all my family were farmers. I saw flying as a natural progression from farming. After you learn the physics of flight, it's just another machine," said Shaffer.

In February 1982, six months before his marriage to Chris, a graduate of Wesleyan's nursing program, Shaffer joined the air force and attended officer training school. He went on to complete Strategic Air Command Combat Crew Training in June 1983 on the KC-135 Stratotanker, a core resource for the aerial refueling of military aircraft.

As a navigator assigned to the 97th Air Refueling Squadron based in Blytheville, Arkansas, Shaffer participated in the April 1986 bombing of Libya, code-named Operation El Dorado Canyon. That same year, he and Chris welcomed the birth of their son, David, and Ken was accepted into the pilot training program.

The path to the cockpit took a short detour during an air force physical. Shaffer's sitting height exceeded military requirements. A second opinion from a doctor who advised Shaffer to "just relax and don't sit up really tall" determined the candidate to be half an inch under the requirement.

Shaffer's fondness for flying traces back to airplane rides he took with his uncle on his birthday. "My interest in aviation began there," he said.

Assignments followed at Castle Air Base in California before he was deployed as a copilot for Central Command at Robins Air Force Base, Georgia. During Desert Shield and Desert Storm, shortly after upgrading to aircraft commander of a KC135R tanker, Shaffer was deployed to bases in Riyadh, Saudi Arabia, and Mont-de-Marsan, France, to fly air refueling missions for coalition aircraft.

After Desert Storm, Shaffer became instructor aircraft commander for CENTCOM EC-135 N/Y. As trip coordinator with diplomatic clearance, Shaffer flew General Norman Schwarzkopf and other high-ranking officers to their destinations.

Mountain Home Air Force Base in Idaho was home for the Shaffers for six months in 1992–93 as he served with the 22nd Air Refueling Squadron, his final assignment in active duty with the air force.

The decision to retire from active duty still stirs an emotional response. After being on "active duty" for more than twelve years, Shaffer needed to turn his attention to his wife and third-grade son. A decision was made to settle down closer to home and have a more stable family life.

When asked if his son was interested in aviation or the military, Shaffer said his son told him, "Dad, don't take this personally but...." The retired aviator turned to his wife to finish the sentence, the words catching in his throat. "He said he wanted to be home more for his family and not gone for long periods of time," said Chris.

Shaffer's military commitment did not end with his retirement. Nine years as a reservist with the 74th Air Refueling Squadron at Grissom Air Force Base in southern Indiana included service with NATO's Combined Air Operations Center during Operation Decisive Endeavor as part of an international peacekeeping mission in the former Yugoslav Republic of Bosnia-Herzegovina.

On September 11, 2001, duty called again. Like most Americans, Shaffer has specific memories of the morning the United States was attacked. "I was driving, on my way to Fort Wayne, for a physical. Chris was watching TV and called with the news."

Right: Shaffer after his first jet aircraft solo flight in the Northrop T-38 Talon.

Below: Ken Shaffer flanked by Master Sargent Scott Ward and Major Brian Stopher.

Images of a second plane crashing into the World Trade Center in New York were on the screen at the doctor's office. Later that afternoon, Shaffer's unit was activated. "It was really eerie because all the traffic control was shut down. We were the only ones in the air," Shaffer said of the refueling operations.

Several days later, Shaffer was deployed as part of allied forces involved in Noble Eagle and Enduring Freedom in the Middle East. The air refueling operations included "fighter drags," a maneuver that allows the air tankers to refuel other planes for the long flights across the Atlantic Ocean.

Shaffer logged 5,500 hours as a command pilot and an additional 20,000 hours with UPS before his retirement in 2020.

Shaffer's collection of military and civilian aviation memorabilia made the retired pilot a popular speaker in his daughter-in-law's elementary school classroom. He also brightened the lives of young students at Schwenksville, Pennsylvania, during Desert Storm. His reply to one student brought letters from every youngster in the class. The handwritten notes wishing him well are still part of Shaffer's collection.

The Waynesville native retired as a major and U.S. Air Force command pilot with more than twenty-one years of service. After twelve years of active duty, Shaffer was looking for a commercial pilot's position. The call came in January 1998 from United Parcel Service. Shaffer and his family were living in central Indiana at the time. Shaffer also was serving as an air force reservist with the 74th Air Refueling Squadron at Grissom Air Force Base.

Cargo Hauling Across the Globe

Shaffer started as flight engineer and copilot before working his way up to captain on Boeing 747 international hauls. He was one of about 2,800 pilots to fly the carrier's 289 airplanes.

The new job required Shaffer to catch a flight from UPS operations in nearby Louisville, Kentucky, for Anchorage, Alaska, where his international flights would begin.

To have eight consecutive days at home, Shaffer spent ten to twelve days on the road—most of that time in the air between Asia and Alaska. The first two days at home were spent recovering from sixteen-hour days on the job. The work schedule and time zone changes, said Shaffer, "are hard on the body."

Shaffer (*center*) on the day of his last flight for UPS, flanked by First Officers Lizzie Eriksson and Ryan Adams.

A typical workweek could take Shaffer from Anchorage to Hong Kong, Shanghai, Honolulu and Seoul before continuing to Bangkok, Mumbai and Dubai. Then it was on to the European UPS hub of Cologne, Germany. Depending on his schedule, he would return via the same destinations to Asia or fly west to the hub at Louisville, Kentucky.

A pilot has eighteen to twenty-four hours of rest at each destination. The break affords pilots "a chance to see a little of the town, have a couple meals, rest and go to the next airport," said Shaffer.

The spread of the COVID-19 pandemic in 2020 became increasingly worrisome for Shaffer and other pilots whose routes included Asian cities. The precautions taken to protect pilots who stayed in Asian hotels did little to alleviate those concerns. In 2020, the threat of COVID-19 and the ongoing updates to technology in the UPS Boeing fleet convinced Shaffer, at age sixty, that "the timing was good to retire."

The Shaffers have settled into their country home, designed by their son, who is an architect. Situated on a secluded acreage surrounded by mature trees, the home is next door to Shaffer's father.

JOHN WARNER

PRIVATE PILOT

As far back as he can remember, John Warner has always wanted to fly. He grew up at a time when World War II aviators were celebrated heroes, and the Space Race was in full swing. At age eight or nine, sporting a toy space helmet, John was already practicing flight maneuvers and bailouts on his swing set. He was not particularly surprised when his mother mentioned in passing that she had personally known many of the famous pilots he was reading about.

"After all," recalled John, "when you're a kid, your parents know all kinds of important people. They know Santa Claus, the Easter Bunny and the Tooth Fairy."

It was only many years later that John learned that his mom's first husband, Joe Hartranft, was one of the three pilots who founded the Aircraft Owners and Pilots Association (AOPA). As an aviation lobbyist, Hartranft, accompanied by his bright and charming young wife, regularly socialized with the likes of Charles and Anne Lindbergh, helicopter pioneer Igor Sikorsky and military aviator Jimmy Doolittle.

In 1983, John was living on a farm near Clinton, Illinois He was taking a break from mowing and enjoying a glass of water in his kitchen when he noticed the sounds of an approaching helicopter. The chopping sounds seemed to circle ever closer until it felt like the whole house was shaking with the downwash. John rushed out of the house and approached the enormous Chinook twin-rotor helicopter that had just landed in his backyard.

John fueling his Stearman at Hooterville Airport.

He recalled, "I thought they'd had an accident, somebody on board had had a heart attack or some sort of emergency." When he reached the helicopter, out of the pilot's window popped the helmeted head of his friend and Vietnam War helicopter pilot Chick Harrington, casually inquiring, "Can we use the phone?"

Harrington was part of a logging crew ferrying a helicopter from Washington State to South Carolina. Since he was passing over his native Illinois, he decided to visit with family and friends. Chick intended to land in Champaign, Illinois, but he did not have the proper sectional chart or the radio frequency to contact the control tower, so he decided to pay his friend John a visit and see if he could use the phone. On his way back to the helicopter, Chick invited John to join him on the short flight to Champaign.

John had always held Chick Harrington in extremely high regard as a military hero and exceptionally gifted pilot. "That day I was hooked," said John. "I had to learn to fly."

As a young clerk at his family's bank, John remembers frequently waiting on retired aviator and former barnstormer "Red" Irwin. John's father often described him as "one of those harum-scarum pilots." The colorful aviator owned a property in rural Hallsville that included his home and a private airstrip. Red had started the airstrip in 1928 when he landed on a portion of the family farm.

In the 1960s, Red was working for Gulf Oil, where his colleagues teased him about living in the boondocks. They jokingly referred to his home base as "Hooterville," a name they borrowed from the popular *Green Acres* sitcom. The series revolved around an affluent and sophisticated New York couple moving to a remote farm community. Red played along with the joke and officially registered his airstrip as "Hooterville Airport."

After learning that John had recently earned his pilot's certificate, Red approached him with a proposition: "I've given up flying, my wife and I are getting old, and we're thinking of moving to town. We've enjoyed our house at Hooterville, and we think you would enjoy it too."

John, who owned a Cessna 150 at the time and had recently inherited the family bank and business, acquired the property and rehabilitated the airstrip that Red had plowed up when he stopped flying.

John has always been drawn to biplanes and open-cockpit flying. While he became proficient in the latest flight instrumentation and navigation technology and owned several modern airplanes, his interest always turned to old-time flying. "The World War II generation of flyers were just about the coolest people around, and those aircraft were some of the most remarkable machines ever designed. I wanted to know that I could master that level of complexity, and I wanted the approval of a World War II aviator," John explained.

Mid-continent Aircraft Corporation, a company based in Hayti, Missouri, was well known as the leading restorer of Boeing Stearman, a World War II biplane flight trainer. Sold as surplus after the war, they became popular as crop dusters.

John commissioned the restoration of a 1943 Stearman to be configured almost exactly the way it was during the war. To satisfy insurance requirements, John had to log eighteen hours of flight instruction on the Stearman. His instructor was a World War II naval aviator.

Learning to fly the airplane was intimidating and taxing. "The military wanted an aircraft that was demanding and hard to fly because it would really teach the new pilots. When you taxi in that tail-wheel airplane, the big radial engine blocks the pilot's view of what's ahead. Imagine getting into your car and having to accelerate to forty miles per hour before you can start to see what's in front of you!"

And so with his gorgeous World War II biplane and a private airstrip, John enjoyed every pilot's ultimate dream. Just like some people might go out

John's World War II Boeing Stearman trainer was a common sight in the sky over Kenney, Illinois.

for a bike ride, John can simply walk out to his backyard airstrip and go for a quick flight. In John's words, "No traffic control, no permission to taxi, it's you making all the decisions—the ultimate freedom!"

Hooterville soon became a social hub for local aviators. Old-time flyers and World War II pilots flew in Wednesday mornings to hang out, drink coffee and swap stories. Over time, the circa 1920s Hooverville ready room was supplemented by a multitude of aviation mementos, flight instruments and gear, charts and barnstormer posters.

John acknowledged that while the sheer joy of flying has never faded, maintaining Hooterville Airport and the Stearman and staying current with his flying certificate was an increasingly heavy commitment. "Here I am with thirty-five years of flying. 1,100 hours in the Stearman with no accidents, I think that's a pretty good career! That decision to stop flying, to no longer go up into the air, is a decision that every pilot must come to grips with. Red Irwin started flying there in 1928, and in a few short years, that airport will be one hundred years old. We're planning a big celebration."

John enjoyed the satisfaction of knowing that just as Red had passed Hooterville on to him, he would be getting ready to pass it on to a third generation.

John unexpectedly passed away in June 2023.

MARK NUNNERY

PRIVATE PILOT

The limitations of Mark Nunnery's eyesight halted his childhood dream of becoming an air force pilot. But his love of aviation and encouragement from a friend steered him toward a pilot's license long after his dream had been set aside. "When I was a youngster, I was fascinated with airplanes and read all kinds of airplane stories. I built all the model planes I could get my hands on. As a young boy, I thought, when I grow up I'm going to join the air force because I'm gonna fly airplanes. And then when I found out you needed 20/20 vision, that kind of ended that little dream."

The allure of aviation stuck with Nunnery as he settled into life with his wife, Gail, and their three daughters on the family farm west of Clinton. The itch to fly flared up after Nunnery's close friend John Warner bought the nearby Hooterville Airport once owned by stunt pilot turned Gulf Oil executive Red Irwin. "This was really the impetus to come out and fly because this long past dream was going to be fulfilled."

Nunnery recalled his first flight in Warner's Cessna 152. Taking off from Hooterville, heading north across the rural landscape, the pilot turned to avoid a grain elevator. "It's almost a euphoric feeling," said Nunnery. As the two sat in Hooterville's ready room after the flight, Warner took out a logbook with records of his time in the air and the plane's maintenance history. Nunnery was shocked to see Malcolm Nunnery, his dad's first cousin from Texas, listed as the pilot who had signed off on an annual maintenance inspection of Warner's plane. "I thought, 'I've got a person in the family who is involved in this. If they can do it, so can I.' And I made the commitment to go to flight school," said Nunnery.

Mark Nunnery.

The nearest flight school was in Lincoln, just a few miles from Nunnery's farm. Former World War II pilot Vinny White, known as Whitey, was Nunnery's instructor. The farmer was eager to learn. "I went at least twice a week, if not more. After the farmwork was done, I made a beeline to Lincoln. We would fly around in the little Piper. I wanted to get it done and get my license."

During his pilot check ride, Nunnery briefly forgot Whitey's last-minute advice to keep his hand on the throttle during the flight. The *wham wham* of the wheels bouncing on the runway didn't cost Nunnery his license, but the check pilot's final words stayed with the new pilot. "He told me, 'You've got your license. Now you're a pilot. Now your learning begins.'"

With flight school behind him, Nunnery went looking for a plane—a mechanically sound aircraft for a reasonable price. After trips to Texas and Missouri to look at planes, he chose a Cessna 172G, built in 1966 and priced at $11,500 in Joliet.

Nunnery still remembers the maiden flight home as exhilarating and nerve wracking, navigating "a scud run around the clouds." "It's not like getting in a new car. You turn on the key and you know how to drive. This is all different. Every plane has its own idiosyncrasies, and you know that going in." When he landed his new plane for the first time, Nunnery was "grinning from ear to ear."

The plane was housed at Hooterville until 1990, when Nunnery completed work on a hangar, designed as part of a new machine shed. Next came the Nunnery Restricted Landing Area, nearly half a mile of grass and oats mowed down close enough to be used as a landing strip.

Nunnery's neighbors were fascinated with the new airfield. For some, it conjured up memories of Irwin's landings in the 1920s across the road from Nunnery's farm. "They'd hear me take off or land and go outside in the yard and watch. Sometimes they would pull up a chair. I would go up for an hour almost every evening. That was my relaxation."

The Nunnery family flew to nearby airports for Sunday morning breakfasts, and then there was the trip to Kentucky's Rough River State Park. It was common for the Nunnery girls to fall asleep in the backseat at some point after takeoff.

The Cessna also came in handy for crop scouting, said Nunnery. "The drones are the big thing now and I'm sure they're great, but it doesn't compare with what you see with your own eyes. I could tell when I had insect

The Nunnerys' 1966 Cessna 172G.

damage or wind damage. I could tell if I missed a strip with anhydrous—those things you don't see from the ground."

Federal rules for private planes require an inspection by an FAA-licensed mechanic after every one hundred hours of flight time or every twelve months, whichever comes first. For a private pilot, one hundred hours is a substantial amount of time in the air, especially when compared to the thousands of hours logged by professional pilots.

Nunnery took his plane to Hooterville, where Jim Schrum, a skilled mechanic with his Airframe and Powerplant licenses, could certify Nunnery's tune-up of the plane and supervise the work, if needed.

With three girls moving closer to their college years, the increased cost of owning the plane called for some tough decisions. An Iowa family with a daughter who was eager to start flying lessons purchased the Cessna. "When they left with that plane, it was just like somebody stabbing me in the heart," Nunnery recalled, his voice heavy with the loss of the aircraft once parked outside his back door.

Nunnery's daughter Sara received a pilot's certification while attending the University of Illinois. She changed her mind about a career in commercial aviation but shared her father's captivation with flight.

Occasional flights with friends stir up memories for Nunnery of his earliest days as a pilot. "I would think to myself, 'You're actually defying the laws of nature. You're defying gravity. You're moving through the air. You're not supposed to be able to do that.'"

ROBB WALTERS

U.S. AIR FORCE MISSILE TRANSPORT

Steady hands and steady nerves were skills Robb Walters honed as a crew member of the U.S. Air Force team tasked with loading Air Intercept Missiles onto F-15 fighter jets.

Walters was in the driver's seat of the truck, known as a Jammer, that transported missiles at Kadena Air Force Base in Okinawa, Japan. Known as the "keystone of the Pacific," the base is the largest air force base in East Asia. Walter's three-member crew with the 18th AGS/67th AMU picked up weapons that were strapped onto a table for the drive to an aircraft. One crew member walked beside the missile, his hand steadying the weapon. To describe the work (all completed by hand) as a delicate task would be an understatement. "If there was any stray electricity to set the motor off, I would be fried," said Walters, who served from 1986 to 1990. The crew was comfortable working together, and each was able to anticipate how each person did his job, a familiarity that inspired confidence during the sensitive operation.

Robb Walters in the cockpit of an F-15 during his 1986 training at Lowry Air Force Base.

Walters was trained on the F-15 weapons systems, including munitions, bombs and missiles. The highly specialized training and attention to detail were evident when a wire needed to be inserted into a single hole the size of a pencil lead in a Mark 82 bomb. "Some of that detail work is what I loved the most," said Walters.

Walters spent the final eighteen months of his military career with the 561st Fighter Squadron at George Air Force Base in Southern California, loading weapons on the F-4 Phantom.

After completing his service, Walters took advantage of the Illinois Veterans Grant Program. He is employed by the Illinois Lottery.

JENNIFER AURORA

ILLINOIS AIR NATIONAL GUARD

Jennifer Aurora and her best friend were curious about the benefits the military had to offer high school graduates in 1989 when they signed up for a weekend with the Illinois Army National Guard.

The army's version of the weekend warrior program was not a good fit for the Bloomington, Illinois teens. Undeterred by that opinion, the best friend's father, a sergeant major with the Army Guard, took the pair to visit the Illinois Air National Guard.

Both graduates signed agreements to serve six years in exchange for a tuition-free college degree and other benefits. "To say my parents were stunned and surprised when I came home that evening is an understatement," said Aurora.

Chief Master Sergeant Jennifer Aurora.

Thirty-five years later, with two war zone deployments behind her, Aurora is the first woman to serve as command chief for the Illinois Air National Guard. Her duties include advising and counseling the adjutant general, assistant adjutant general for air and wing commanders on concerns of the three-thousand-member enlisted force.

The fact that Aurora began her military commitment during peacetime faded as a consolation for her parents when soldiers were summoned for Operation Desert Storm. The deployment followed training at air force bases in Texas and Mississippi. Personnel was her career choice. In 1999, Aurora was offered a position as a full-time active guard reserve member. She left her civilian job for a post on the 183rd Wing Headquarters command support staff.

Aurora ran the Operation Orderly Room during her first deployment in 2004 to Al Udeid, Qatar. She recalled quickly learning the skills needed to keep track of flights in and out of the region. During her second deployment in 2006 to Balad, Iraq, Aurora supervised myriad operations—everything from flights to mail delivery—as the noncommissioned officer in charge of operations. "You're every job when you're deployed, usually working seven days a week," said the command chief.

The camaraderie of the deployments is among Aurora's favorite IANG experiences. A military woman's experience differs from that of her male counterparts at home and abroad. In Iraq, Aurora's work with injured children caught in the crossfire put her in close contact with parents unaccustomed to seeing a woman in uniform, her bare arms exposed to the scorching desert temperatures. For parents coming to visit their children in the makeshift medical facilities, "it was a difficult culture shock."

In Illinois, Aurora's work as command chief of the 183rd Wing in Springfield served as an example to other female guard members. Hairstyle regulations relaxed during the pandemic allowed women to wear their hair in ponytails, a change from the rules that required long hair to be worn in a bun. "It's about time," Aurora said of the rule change. Others agree.

During a visit to Scott Air Force base in southern Illinois, female guard members noticed Aurora's blonde locks gathered in a ponytail. "Way to represent, Chief," they cheered.

When it comes to minorities who have served in the commanding role, Aurora stands alone. "I believe we still have a lot of ground to cover when it comes to getting more minorities into leadership roles," she said.

With the commitment of being a citizen soldier comes the demands of everyday life and what it means to be called to active duty without warning. Aurora said, "One of the most challenging parts of serving in any capacity in the military is the balance between work and family."

One of Aurora's overseas junkets took her to Poland as part of the Department of Defense's State Partnership Program, a program that links National Guard elements with partners worldwide. As one of the first participants in the program, Illinois' relationship with Poland dates back to 1993. Aurora was the only female guard member on the joint training mission.

Aurora sits in the cockpit of a Mikoyan-Gurevich MiG-21 during a Department of Defense partnership program trip to Poland.

What started as a weekend commitment once a month for a fledgling volunteer flourished into a career and the highest rank for a woman in the IANG's seventy-five-year history. Retirement had crossed Aurora's mind. But at the border of that decision to retire in March 2023 was a hesitancy to leave a position she loved and people she respected. "The uniform represents how I define myself and how the community defines my role," she said.

ANDREW NEWBERG

COMMERCIAL PILOT

Andrew Newberg divides his time between the best of two worlds: aviation and agriculture. Newberg planned to join his family's farm operation after college, but a commercial pilot's license wasn't on his radar until a conversation in his dorm with a fellow student at the University of Illinois. "It was my freshman year, and I was talking to a kid who said he was taking flying lessons," said Newberg. After a flight to visit his sister, he told his parents, "I think I'd like to check out this flying thing at the U of I."

Newberg continued to work on a degree in business and finance while studying with the school's aeronautics program. The chaos of 9/11 grounded planes across the country and shuttered airports, including Willard Airport in Champaign, where students were learning to fly. The economic downturn that followed the attacks shrank the market for pilots, along with other job opportunities for graduates.

After graduation, Newberg taught others to fly and worked on the farm east of Clinton. Experience as an instructor at the Bloomington Regional Airport added to the hours Newberg needed for a commercial pilot's license. "Luckily, I was able to bridge the farming with aviation," said Newberg. The young aviator's first corporate flying job was in Champaign, followed by a stint with ADM in Decatur. In 2013, he started as a pilot with Growmark in Bloomington, where he spends about twelve days a month transporting staff with the agricultural firm to locations in the United States and southern Canada.

Andrew Newberg is joined in the cockpit by his sister, Suzy Brown; her children, Luke and Brady Brown; Jack Amiano; and their dog Lucky in a 1976 Piper Lance.

In 2012, the Newbergs added an airplane to the family with the acquisition of a 1976 Piper Lance from Clinton businessman and friend Virgil Harbach. Behind the sprawling red hangar that also serves as an office for the family farm operation is the Sugar Hollow landing strip, installed by Newberg's parents, Joni and David Newberg.

In warm weather, Newberg and his wife, Jill, enjoy taking their two sons on trips aboard the Piper. "We used to put their car seats in the plane, and they'd eat peanut butter and jelly sandwiches on the trip," said Newberg. The joy of aviation never seems to wear off. "I've been pretty blessed to be able to fly," said the Clinton pilot.

MASON KARCZ

U.S. AIR FORCE

Mason Karcz considered other branches of the military before he settled on the U.S. Air Force, a decision that has led to a career working with unmanned aerial vehicles, commonly known as drones. "It was a shotgun decision, but I have enjoyed my career," Karcz said of the move away from his previous focus on the accounting field. After finishing a two-year degree, Karcz "wanted direction, and a sense of belonging, but most importantly I didn't want to move back home with my parents and feel like a failure."

As a technical sergeant based in Nevada, Karcz works for the 432 Aircraft Maintenance (MX) Squadron. "My day-to-day responsibilities include running the flight line, ensuring scheduled MX is tracked and finished on time. I ensure accurate tracking of all aircraft statuses, locations, fuel totals, delayed discrepancies and in-flight emergencies. I am the operations center for all significant events on the flightline," said the Clinton High School graduate.

Four deployments—including two to Afghanistan, one in Turkey and another to Romania—illustrated the multiple roles played by the UAVs in the field. "In Afghanistan, they were used for a more offensive operation, to spy on our enemies, give ground

Opposite: Karcz is doused in aviation fuel during a deployment to Romania.

Above: Karcz at Creech AFB in Nevada.

troops accurate real-time locations of our adversaries and to utilize hellfire missiles/bombs when necessary," said Karcz, offering a general overview of the vehicle's capabilities. In Turkey and Romania, where ammunitions were not authorized, the mission was limited to surveillance.

After nine years, Karcz has earned a second associate's degree and plans to work on a bachelor's degree. He is on his way to having a lifetime pension. "As far as career progression goes, it is very cut and dried: do your job well, be responsible and you'll be promoted. I have been able to obtain my own personal goals while in the air force, so it has been rewarding for me," said Karcz.

RICH RYBOLT

U.S. MARINE HELICOPTER PILOT

Surrounded by his father's drawings of P-51 Mustangs, Rich Rybolt daydreamed of wearing a military uniform to elementary school, an early premonition of his service as a U.S. Marine Corps helicopter pilot in the deserts of Iraq and Afghanistan.

Rybolt's move from the central Illinois farming community of Kenney to Texas offered him a front-row seat to the thrill of military aviation. "I was thirteen or fourteen. There was a B-52 base pretty close, and it was fascinating watching those big planes," said Rybolt.

His enduring love of flying grew from his dad's sketches, his love of video games and what he observed from outside the airfield gates. A career in uniform never left his sights. "I didn't join the Marines until I was twenty-seven and had never flown before. A lot of time had passed since college, and I saw the clock was ticking. I knew it was now or never."

The guarantee of an aviation contract, if he could pass the required tests, put the Marine Corps at the top of Rybolt's list. In the spring of 2001, he became a marine recruit. Several months later, Rybolt was stationed at Quantico, Virginia, when the first plane pierced the side of the World Trade Center in New York. "I was a brand-new second lieutenant, hanging out, watching television in the barracks" when news of the attack was broadcast. "Guys were punching the doors, crying—there was a lot of confusion." He saw fellow marines leaving the base for assignments tied to the U.S. response to the assault on American soil by Osama Bin Laden.

Rybolt finished basic training, where he learned the skills of company commander. Flight school in Pensacola, Florida, followed, with eight weeks

Rich Rybolt.

of intensive training in aerodynamics and the basics of helicopter and fixed-wing aircraft.

Water skills were part of the training. "Everybody has to swim a mile in a flight suit without touching the bottom or the sides. You have to do a survival stroke for a mile. It takes about fifty minutes, and it was difficult. I failed the first time because I wasn't a strong swimmer," Rybolt recalled.

About 25 percent of those who start the training will wash out due to poor test scores, said Rybolt. "It's even more difficult once you get in the airplane." The tough training regimen is behind the reputation of Marine Corps pilots for being aggressive in the field, especially when it comes to helping ground troops and rescue missions, said Rybolt.

Marine Bravado

"Whenever people are calling and they hear they've got Marine Air, they're like, 'That's what we want' because they know we're not pulling some bullshit to get out of the fire, because we like to fight."

For the most part, Rybolt's fellow marines shared similar personalities, work ethics and values. There was also mutual bravado. "A certain personality is drawn to aviation," Rybolt acknowledged. Flight training in Corpus Christi, Texas, put Rybolt in T-34 Mentors. He divided his time between simulators and the single-engine military trainer. Another future bad-ass pilot in a bad-ass plane.

After a series of solo flights, pilots received instrument training—a milestone that ended the flight careers of those who couldn't make the grade. "If you're not gonna be able to do instruments, they don't want to give you a lot of training," said Rybolt. Instructors had a process for weeding out aviators who did not meet military standards. Pilots were positioned in the back seat of the plane, with a hood covering the back portion of the aircraft, forcing trainees to use pressure-driven steam gauges to navigate the plane. "You just have the gauges, and the instructor takes you up and you have to do a litany of instrument exercises with the hood on. A lot of people washed out pretty quickly," Rybolt recalled.

At the end of primary training, pilots were assigned to a specific aircraft—jets, helicopters or C-130s—based on test scores. Rybolt said he narrowly missed jets, "but I ended up liking helicopters."

Rich Rybolt and his helicopter.

Back in Pensacola, Rybolt mastered "a lot of contradictory movements" involved in controlling a chopper. Three main controls require constant, delicate adjustment. The cyclic changes the pitch of the blades, and the collective raises and lowers the aircraft. Add the anti-torque pedals and pilots have a full plate of variables, each with its own role in keeping pilots safe as they perform dangerous missions.

Putting the flyer's complicated skills into simple terms, Rybolt explained, "It's hard work, but it's kind of like riding a bike. It's balance."

On his first deployment in 2006, Rybolt landed at Camp Taqaddum in central Iraq. With its long runway, the former Iraqi base proved a useful military site when it was taken over by the United States in 2003 and served as a major hub for coalition forces during Operation Iraqi Freedom. The 3rd Marine Aircraft Wing provided air support for ground troops and other aircraft. Some days, the roar of the Huey's blades provided the protection needed for caravans moving on the ground.

"If there was rotor noise overhead, the bad guys would leave them alone." The Huey's hovering range was between five hundred and one thousand feet.

Walls of Sand and Death

Rybolt did not consider death an inevitable part of war. But as death made more frequent rounds in the area, the likelihood of not making it home crossed his mind more often. Simple tasks took on an air of perceived destiny. "When I was brushing my teeth, I would find myself wondering, is this the last time I will ever be putting my toothbrush away?"

The names, dates and circumstances of the losses are never forgotten. Rybolt recalled a fellow marine, a rancher from Texas, felled by a sniper round. "When you see those things happen, it brings it home to you. The names just kept adding up."

When an aircraft went down, "It was a huge deal," said Rybolt, and created an immediate response from air and ground troops. A male and female pilot in a CH-46, a smaller version of a Chinook, were felled by a surface-air missile that left their chopper in a backward pitch before landing on its top. The two were transporting a bag of blood when the aircraft went down.

"When that happens, the whole theater lights up. We're in the first layer, and then there's the Quick Reaction Force and the ground guys. We were there as long as we had fuel, taking a lot of indirect fire."

As part of their training, members of Rybolt's unit learned how to fly through the walls of sand that could envelop helicopters during "brown out landings." "One of the highest risks is the brown out landings. They're hard to predict, with how much dust is gonna be there and what the terrain will be like. That's just one of those things you're always prepared for and build your confidence to be able to perform."

The process of refueling helicopters was another risky maneuver requiring confidence, timing and skill. As one chopper was on the ground refueling, one or more would be hitting a target.

During a hot refuel, "You just idle down, get out and stretch or take a leak, and meanwhile the crew is refueling." Onboard missiles were disarmed during the dangerous movement. Fuel in the main and auxiliary tanks gave pilots about two and a half hours in the air.

When on the ground, crews worked to find ways to rest their minds and bodies. Living conditions in the desert amounted to cramped, two-man spaces in the rows of metal-clad housing units known as "cans." The air-conditioned units were a refuge from the intense heat. The other alternative was a canvas tent that lacked any separation between quarters. The food was acceptable, said Rybolt, and even included an occasional steak and lobster meal.

Drones and Tourist Trips

For his final deployment in Afghanistan, Rybolt worked with drones, helping operators determine if other aircraft were in the area. He recalled using a drone's laser designator during a mission to help locate an adversary who fled after setting up an improvised explosive device. "We tracked him for half an hour, running down this old road, and we got an F-18 that just dropped on him. He turned into what's called 'pink mist.'"

While not the assignment he preferred, Rybolt found the drone work less stressful. "I wasn't puckered up all the time. I was able to kind of relax, even though I was deployed."

Through the end of 2019, the conflicts in Afghanistan and Iraq claimed seven thousand troops. The war that started out as retaliation for the 9/11 attacks turned to an elimination effort of weapons of mass destruction held by Iraqi President Saddam Hussein, an allegation later proven to be false.

Soon after his return from Afghanistan, Rybolt was discharged and decided to transition to civilian flight training; he stayed with helicopters, the aircraft he knew best. He was accumulating hours with an instructor in Kansas when a friend offered him a job flying tourists on the Big Island of Hawaii over the Kilauea volcano.

"It was eight flights a day, of forty to forty-five minutes—a little too much work. Then I went to the other side of the island, on a bigger Bell 407. Those were flights of an hour and fifteen minutes, all the way around the island. I would do two or three of those a day."

While Rybolt enjoyed the sightseeing job, he did not enjoy the weather conditions in what amounted to almost a dozen climate conditions on one island, everything from snow-capped peaks to rainforest conditions. "The weather just about clobbered me a couple of times. Hilo, Hawaii, is the wettest city on the face of the earth, with 140 inches of rain a year, and the other side of the island is pretty dry," Rybolt explained.

Weather patterns and pressure from owners of the sightseeing business to fly choppers that may have benefited from more extensive mechanical checkups caused Rybolt to leave the job after two years. Back in central Illinois, he landed a job with Caterpillar in Decatur, working on the supply side of the manufacturer.

There is no hesitation when the former Marine Corps pilot is asked what he misses most about military service. "The professionalism and the level of camaraderie. It's unparalleled."

CHRIS LAREAU

ILLINOIS NATIONAL GUARD, COMMERCIAL PILOT

Chris Lareau loaded cargo on C-130s for delivery around the world before he decided during a deployment to Afghanistan that he wanted to fly the plane.

Lareau signed up with the Illinois Air National Guard in May 2004 shortly before he graduated from Clinton High School. Military service is a family tradition. First to join was Nicolas, who signed up with the Illinois Air National Guard in 2002 and served as an aerospace medical services technician. Serving as a staff sergeant, he was assigned to the 183rd Medical Group, of the 183rd Fighter Wing, in Springfield. Younger brother Matthew served with the Marine Corps as a jet engine mechanic on F-18s with the VMFA-115 Silver Eagles. Enlisting in the Corps in 2006, Sergeant Lareau was deployed to Iraq in 2008 and Japan one year later.

The military commitments meant successive overseas tours for the siblings. After basic training at Lackland Air Force Base in Texas, Chris Lareau completed training as a C-130 loadmaster. Three deployments followed: Kuwait in 2005 and Afghanistan in 2008 and 2010.

Living conditions varied according to where Lareau was assigned. In Kuwait, "It is worth noting that as a flyer we usually received better living conditions," compared to non-crew members, who lived in tents, said the Clinton native. A day room with a TV, recliners and desktop computers were part of the crew quarters. A gym, pool and "a fairly nice chow hall" were within walking distance on the base.

The Lareau brothers: Nicolas, Chris and Matthew.

Things were different in Afghanistan. The "B-huts," or Barracks Huts, were plywood structures with a main hallway separating four rooms large enough for a twin bed and space to change one's clothes on each side.

In 2011, the dream of learning to fly "really took off while I was working in Afghanistan as a contract loadmaster" with FlightWorks on the de Havilland Caribou DHC-4, said Lareau, now a commercial pilot based in Wyoming.

The Caribou was popular in Vietnam for troop transport and airdrops. The Caribou assigned to the FlightWorks crew was outfitted with upgraded PT-6 engines. A special FAA operations exemption allowed the aircraft to fly 150 feet above ground for airdrop operations, a dramatic change from its normal above-ground limit of 500 feet.

The smaller plane had room for two pilots and the loadmaster, as well as the aviators' stories exchanged between Lareau and the pilots. "I would sit in the jump seat right behind the pilots. Being that close to the action and listening to the stories from the pilots about their other flying jobs led me to pursue the career as a pilot," he said.

During his three years with FlightWorks, Lareau rotated in and out of Afghanistan multiple times in two-month rotations, performing hundreds of low-altitude airdrops to U.S. Special Operations units. "The airdrops usually consisted of fuel, food, water and ammunition. We would even tie care packages from the Red Cross into the airdrop bundles for the guys in the field."

Most of Lareau's training for his private, multi-engine, instrument and commercial rating was completed at Rocky Mountain Flight School in

Chris Lareau working as loadmaster on the de Havilland Caribou DHC-4 in Afghanistan.

Broomfield, Colorado. In 2012, he transferred to the Wyoming Air National Guard in Cheyenne. He qualified to work with the Modular Airborne Fire Fighting Systems, a special mission performed by four C-130 units in the National Guard and reserve units.

Small dirt landing strips in Uganda, South Somalia and the Central African Republic were ahead for Lareau in 2017 when he took a job as copilot for defense contractor Erickson Inc. Cargo, passengers and food were taken to small bases in Africa.

Tourists looking to scratch an adventure from their bucket lists were among the passengers in the Cessna 206 piloted by Lareau over the Grand Canyon for Paragon Skydive and the Cessna 182 for Rocky Mountain Skydive in Colorado. "We would fly near the Grand Canyon so they could get a good view on the way up and then drop them over the Grand Canyon Airport. I was able to jump once when another pilot was there to help with the flying, and it was a thrill," Lareau recalled.

Lareau went from dropping skydivers in the Lower 48 to smokejumpers in Alaska in 2018 with Big Horn Airways. As copilot of a CASA 212, Lareau was on call for the U.S. Forest Service and Bureau of Land Management to fly smokejumpers and cargo to firefighting forces on the ground.

"Everything is on very short notice with this kind of operation," said Lareau. "All of the smokejumpers and pilots are on the smokejumper base, and when an alarm goes off and an announcement is made, the smokejumpers rush to their lockers and get their gear as quickly as possible and the pilots head straight to the plane."

The intense schedule required the planes to be pre-flighted and ready to go at all times. Food, water, chainsaws, hoses and axes were preloaded. "We basically just needed to get into the seat and start running checklists," Lareau said of the assignment. Once over the fire, the pilots would make several passes, and smokejumpers would throw out streamers to determine the best release point. Once on the ground, the smokejumpers would radio the plane and let the crew know what cargo they needed to be dropped from the aircraft.

After he was commissioned as an officer, Lareau graduated in 2019 from U.S. Air Force undergraduate pilot training at Vance Air Force Base in Oklahoma. The yearlong course included experience flying the T-6 Texan II and the T-1. After initial and mission qualification training in Arkansas on the C-130, Lareau returned to the Wyoming Air Guard, where he has served as a captain and copilot on the aircraft since 2020.

These days, Lareau divides his time between the Wyoming Air National Guard and work as a first officer for PSA Airlines, a regional airline owned by American Airlines, flying the CRJ 700/900 aircraft.

COLE NEWMAN

U.S. AIR FORCE RESERVES

Inspiration from his younger brother steered Cole Newman to the U.S. Marine Corps in 2012 after he finished a two-year degree with no clear career path ahead of him. "My brother Blake had mentioned his interest in joining the military, and I couldn't allow him to do something cooler than me. So, being the highly competitive person I am, I enlisted right away," said Newman. With his active-duty enlistment behind him in 2017, Newman worked two years climbing cellphone towers and working in the IT field.

The call to military service rang once again in Newman's ear. "I got the itch to get back into uniform," he said, "but I wasn't so sure about going active duty again, so I knew I wanted to join the reserves." This time, Newman's inspiration was his close friend from Clinton, Mason Karcz, who is serving with the U.S. Air Force's 432 Aircraft Maintenance Squadron. "I like the idea of trying something new, and I also loved aviation. So, with those things in mind, I talked to the air force about flying in some capacity." After some research, he became hooked on being a load master for the air force reserves.

Cole Newman.

Newman on a mission to deliver COVID-19 supplies to India.

Here's how Newman explained the work: "My job on a daily basis was to plan and coordinate the movement of personnel and assets around the world. As a loadmaster, it is our sole duty to make sure that we can configure the load of our aircraft to handle the weight and stresses of the cargo we are carrying abroad. We complete complicated mathematical computations to make sure that we do not exceed the limitations of the aircraft, as well as getting the crew to our objective safely. As a loadmaster, it is also our duty to provide protection for others on the aircraft. We were trained in using small arms to provide a sense of security for our flight crew; we are one of the few positions that are armed on the aircraft."

Newman served from 2019 to 2022 as a flight deck loadmaster. Among his assignments was a 2020 trip to India to deliver COVID-19 relief supplies. During the stop at Gandhi International Airport, the crew met with local health groups.

Now living in Texas, where he works as a radar technician for Raytheon Technologies, Newman considers the military "a great career for anyone who wants to challenge themselves as well as make an impact in a career."

The experience "forces people to mature quickly and figure out what kind of person they truly are here."

Newman looks back at his time with the U.S. Air Force with gratitude but admits that "my heart will always be with the Marine Corps for giving me my upbringing into the military and helping me grow in ways I didn't know I needed. The air force was a nice change, but I will always claim the title of marine first."

VICTORIA MASKE-MENDENALL AND MONICA HAWKINS

GROUND CREW

Travelers passing through Decatur Airport are likely to have their bags checked and loaded onto a plane by a female member of the ground crew for SkyWest Airlines.

Victoria Maske-Mendenall and Monica Hawkins are among eleven women who work on the eighteen-member ground crew at the airport that serves DeWitt and surrounding counties in central Illinois. Analise McDonald is station manager for the airline's Decatur operation.

Maske-Mendenall, a supervisor who started with the airline in January 2020, was attracted to the employee flight benefits, like free standby tickets on all United flights. Air travel has always been something she enjoyed.

The part-time job turned into full-time with more responsibilities for making certain the plane is cleaned between flights and safe to leave the ground. Among the crew's cold weather duties is deicing the plane, a task that takes them high in the air in a bucket truck to reach the wings and tails. In grade school, Hawkins dreamed of being an astronaut. But law school led her to a stressful courtroom job. The part-time ground crew position is a stress reliever. "When I walk in here, the stress just melts away," said Hawkins.

Hawkins also has the chance to marshal planes onto the tarmac and build a few more muscles by loading luggage weighing up to fifty pounds onto the aircraft. "We do everything but fly the planes," said Hawkins.

The crew works closely with federal TSA agents who inspect the contents of luggage before it boards the plane. A group of airport workers waiting

Victoria Maske and Monica Hawkins.

for the arrival of an afternoon flight had multiple stories about some of the items discovered inside suitcases. McDonald will never forget the bag of crawfish tucked inside a bag. Then there was the live lizard—not allowed on an aircraft—and a hunter's severed deer head that an agent cleared for transport.

SkyWest had just opened its Decatur base when COVID-19 brought air travel to a near standstill in 2020. "There was a rush of people trying to get home before the borders shut down," recalled Maske-Mendenall.

As time passed, fewer people were willing to board planes. On a trip to O'Hare International Airport in Chicago with her daughter, Maske-Mendenall saw one passenger in three hours in the web of terminals that normally handle thousands of passengers per day.

In 2021, about eight thousand passengers passed through Decatur Airport as the facility and others across the globe inched toward recovery from the impacts of the pandemic. Daily airport traffic comes from two incoming and two departing flights per day.

After four years, McDonald still appreciates that no two days are alike at the airport. "Once it gets in your blood, you stick with it. Every day brings something new," she said.

ABOUT THE AUTHORS

EDITH BRADY-LUNNY (*left*) is a former print and broadcast journalist. She is the coauthor of *The Unforgiven: The Untold Story of One Woman's Search for Love and Justice*. She is a journalism fellow at John Jay College of Criminal Justice Center on Media, Crime and Justice in New York. She resides with her family in Central Illinois.

DENIS HAMBUCKEN (*center*) is an author, designer, photographer, illustrator and advertising professional with a passion for history. Originally from Belgium, he now resides in New Hampshire.

JOHN WARNER (*right*) dedicated his life to the preservation of agriculture in the Midwest and a passion for history. His childhood love of aviation continued throughout his years as a pilot. Born in Central Illinois, he divided his time between the Hooterville Airport in Hallsville, Illinois, and his home in New Hampshire. He was a gifted writer. John's life ended tragically in a June 2023 accident in New Hampshire.